TRUTH ABOUT MARRIAGE

EVALUATION EXERCISE WORKBOOK

By

JAMES JR HAIRSTON

INTRODUCTION

In this book are the four major truths about marriage coupled with practical exercises to enhance your relationship with our mate. The husband and the wife will be able to evaluate their marriage while participating in the exercises. Yet, it will become more challenging and interesting by incorporating group interaction. Moreover, with the evaluation a score is created for your marriage. How exciting! Enhance your marriage to whatever level you choose. The sky is the limit. It is up to how serious you are about your marriage and what you decide to do. However, there is a cost, and that will be based on truth about marriage, and it will take some work to accomplish whatever goals you may have for your marriage. The cost is simply your time, energy, and commitment. The commitment is not to Truth About Marriage and family and marriage enrichment, it is to God!

What is truth about marriage?

Truth about marriage is four major truths that are critical to your spiritual growth and marital enrichment.

- Truth is a person, and that person is Jesus Christ. He said, "I am the way and the truth and the life. No one comes to the Father except through me." Jo. 14:6.
- Truth about marriage is Jesus at the center.
- Jesus is the first to know and the last to know – the alpha and the omega, the beginning and the end.
- God's Word is where He speaks to us through the Holy Spirit, Jo.16: 13.

Truth about marriage is five major parts that are significant to God's awesome marital design.

1. Truth about marriage is the image and likeness of God's Kingdom/Church – Gen. 2:9, 15-17, 23, 24, and Eph. 5:22-33.
2. Truth about marriage is oneness between one man and one woman – Gen. 2:24, Eph. 5:31, I Cor. 7:3-5.
3. Truth about marriage is purity in the home – Gen. 2:25, Ro. 8:9 (man and woman did not see the flesh in the beginning and we

should not live and view each other in the flesh either), and Lev. 11:44, 20:7.

4. Truth About marriage is holy communication Pr. 12: 15, Pr. 29: 18, Pr.18: 21, Pr. 6: 2-3, Matt. 6: 12, 14, 15, II Co. 12: 13, Matt. 5: 23. Life and Death is in power of the tongue and forgiveness needs to be spoken to one another instead of 'I am sorry'.

5. Truth about Marriage is building a family to subdue and have dominion over the earth – Gen. 1:28, Eph. 1:3, 2:6, Jo.16: 33, I Jo. 5:4, 6, Ro 8:21 and Matt 11: 12 (the Kingdom of God is being established by force or in the KJV, "violently"). These are major truths and we need to go more in depth.

If one of these truths is not present in our marriages, we miss out experiencing God in our marriage in a powerful way.

If you are not experiencing the Truth about Marriage, you may encounter

Separation from God
Depression
Guilt
Family marital problems
Denial of family marital problems
Drugs and alcoholism
Psychosomatic problems
Poor decision making
Child rearing problems
Sexual problems

Communication problems
Sexual immorality
Adultery
Lack of joy
Lack of peace and happiness
Lack of affection
Financial problems
Unity problems
Lack of faith, hope, and many other things

Do any of these hit home? Are you and your spouse seeking more out of your relationship? Is your marriage in need of salvation? Marriage is based on truth, and truth is a person. *Jesus answered, "I am the way and the truth and the life. No one comes to the Father except through me." Jo. 14: 6 NIV.*

Truth about Marriage will Teach you How To

- Love your wife as Christ loves the Church.
- Be heads of your households.
- Submit to your own husbands.

- Use the bible to determine your convictions, decisions, and practices in life in general and marriage in particular.
- Study the bible, pray, worship God, and seek to serve God together.
- Seek to please one another.
- Ask for forgiveness when you have done something wrong (not just saying I am sorry).
- Focus on the things you appreciate about your mate and express appreciation in tangible ways.
- Have biblical communication and to communicate on a daily basis.
- Be excited with each other.
- Show love in many different tangible and practical ways.
- Court one another by occasional gifts, unexpected attention etc.
- Have pleasant and friendly conversations.
- Pray for one another. Support and seek to encourage one another.
- Anticipate sexual relationships with your partner to have heavenly sex. (Set your affections on things above, not on things on the earth – Col. 3:2)
- Be as one with finances
- Multiply, subdue and build God's Kingdom/having dominion over the earth.

God Hates Divorce [Mal. 2:16]

"I hate divorce," says the Lord God of Israel, "and I hate a man's covering himself with violence as well as with his garment," says the Lord Almighty, NIV.

Experience God in the total capacity of your mind

*"Jesus replied, Love the Lord your God with all your heart and with all your soul and with all your **mind**. This is the first and greatest commandment. And the second is like it. 'Love your neighbor as yourself,' 'Matthew 22:37-39', NIV."*

The mind, in its entirety, means the full faculty of your mind. Every extent of space with all your strength! To love God **habitually** means to really love Him. Habitual love is a continual love formed by habit, or loving God by acting in love spiritually that becomes natural or habit-forming! Loving God in the Spirit by habit only comes from God supernaturally. Supernatural love comes from what you have stored in your mind about how to love God under His supernatural power by

His Holy Spirit, not of your own. Love is not phony; to put it on or only to love back is to form habits of practicing God's Word continually to love God with our whole self! Therefore, In turn we will, I quote, "we will love our spouses **habitually**" – "The second is like it, Love your neighbor as yourself!"

1. **Let us practice Habitual Agape Love in our Marriage as the Image and Likeness of God's Kingdom**

You will have to recognize who you are as a believer in your home as the Church. In Romans 16:16 it says to greet one another with a holy kiss. As the Church of Christ, I challenge you to greet one another with a holy kiss and a hug in your home daily! (Hugs are part of American culture.) This is one example of what the Church looks like in fellowship.

2. **Let us practice Habitual Agape Love in our Marriage as Oneness**
   What is sex like in your marriage?

Are you compatible? God intended it for enjoyment.

How many times a week or times per month is your relationship filled with sex, or in modern day language 'making love'? Wives, are you satisfied? Do you look forward to the next sexual encounter with your mate?

3. **Let us practice Habitual Agape Love in our Marriage as Purity**

Ask yourself how you see your mate:

❑In the flesh
❑In the Spirit
❑As a wonderful precious spiritual being

Check all the boxes that apply, Romans 8:9.

How we view our mate is the result of our treatment towards them. We must be able to see them in the Spirit while under pressure, in an argument, disagreements, and heated discussions. In addition, how we see them when we make a mistake or sin has a lasting effect. Keep these things in mind when you conduct your evaluation.

4. **Let us practice Habitual Agape love in our Marriage as building God's Kingdom to subdue and have dominion over the earth.**

What are we doing to advance the Kingdom with our money and time? Are we experiencing God in our marriages and teaching it in our communities, and showing the world what God's Kingdom looks like in our homes and marriages? God said to multiply, build families, subdue, and have dominion over the earth. Therefore, we need to be teaching people how great God's Kingdom is in marriage and be excited about it – experiencing it!

SCRIPTURE READING

John 15: 4

"Remain in me, and I will remain in you. No branch can bear fruit by itself; it must remain in the vine. Neither can you bear fruit unless you remain in me." **NIV**

UNIT I

EVALUATE YOUR MARRIAGE

EVALUATE YOUR MARRIAGE

MEMORY VERSE

I Corinthians 11: 31
"But if we judged ourselves, we would not come under judgment." NIV.

EVALUATE YOUR MARRIAGE

In this unit, we are going to have fun expressing and showing love to our mates. However, you will spot problem areas so that you may work on correcting them. While having fun taking this evaluation, you need to be serious and sensitive to your mate's needs. The evaluation will be most beneficial if both spouses take it, then sit down and discuss your respective answers to each question. In doing so, seek to understand clearly the other person's reasons for answering each question as it is written. Here is where we really need to focus on resolving any issues **biblically**. Remember to have fun with the evaluation, yet learning from one another, allowing God to use you to glorify Him. Do not attack each other because of some difficult point of views keep your focus on God and don't get off track. Possess the fruits of the Spirit, Gal. 5:22. **Sit down together, get on your knees, and start to pray before conducting this evaluation!**

Galatians 5: 22

"But the fruit of the Spirit is love, joy, peace, longsuffering, gentleness [kindness], goodness, faith [faithfulness], Meekness, temperance: against such there is no law." KJV

Rating Scale: Never = 0➢ Seldom = 1➢ Sometimes = 2➢ Frequently = 3➢ Always = 4

Here are the equations for the scores

Scores: 140 = Perfect or Idea➢ 95-139 = you're experiencing unity and happiness➢ 70-94 = Need for improvement

Workshop one

EVALUATION BEGINS

Write your desired number in the box next to the question. Then write your explanation for your answers on the lines provided. After examining yourself primarily on each question, write the evaluation score of your spouse in the box next to yours. Allow the Holy Spirit to work in your evaluations and discussions.

Does the fact that Jesus Christ is Lord manifest itself in practical ways in your marriage? ☐☐

_____

_____

_____

Do you use the Bible to determine your convictions, decisions, and practices in life in general and marriage in particular? ☐☐

_____

_____

_____

Do you and your spouse study the Bible, pray, worship God, and seek to serve God together? ☐☐

_____

_____

_____

Do you and your spouse seek to please one another? ☐☐

_____

_____

Do you ask forgiveness when you have done something wrong? ☐☐

_____

_____

_____

Do you allow your mate to disagree with you or make a mistake without becoming nasty or punishing them? ☐☐

_____

_____

_____

Do you focus on the things you appreciate about your mate and express appreciation in tangible ways? ☐☐

_____

_____

_____

Do you communicate with one another on a daily basis? ☐☐

_____

_____

_____

Do you express your opinions, ideas, plans, aspirations, fears, feelings, likes, etc. to each other? ☐☐

_____

_____

_____

Do you and your mate understand each other when you try to express yourselves? ☐☐

_____

_____

_____

Do you do many different things together and enjoy being with each other? ☐☐

_____

_____

_____

Do you show love in many practical and tangible ways? ☐☐

_____

_____

_____

Do you still court one another with occasional gifts, unexpected attention, etc? ☐☐

_____

_____

Is your conversation pleasant and friendly? ☐☐

Do you pray for one another, support, and seek to encourage one another? ☐☐

Can you discuss differing viewpoints, values, and priorities, etc. without becoming irritated? ☐☐

Do you anticipate sexual relations with your partner? ☐☐

Are your sexual desires compatible? ☐☐

Do you freely discuss your sexual desires with your mate? ☐☐

Do you agree about the way money should be spent? ☐☐

Do you think your spouse is as concerned about your views on money as you are? ☐ ☐

Do you agree on how to bring up your children? ☐ ☐

Do your children know that it is foolish to try to play one of you against the other? ☐ ☐

Do you refuse to lie to your spouse; are you building your relationship on speaking the truth? ☐ ☐

Do you have a good relationship with your in-laws? ☐ ☐

Do you really respect your spouse? ☐ ☐

Are you glad to introduce your spouse to friends and associates? ☐ ☐

Do you control yourself when you are moody so that you do not disrupt your family? ☐☐

Do you seek to change your specific habits that may cause discomfort to your spouse? ☐☐

Do you make your relationship with your spouse a priority? ☐☐

Do you treat your mate with respect and dignity? ☐☐

Do you accept corrective criticism graciously? ☐☐

Do you agree concerning the role and responsibilities of the husband and wife? ☐☐

Are you willing to face, discuss, and look for scriptural solutions to problems without blowing up or attacking the other person? ☐☐

_____

_____

_____

Do you maintain your own spiritual life through Bible study, prayer, regular church attendance, and fellowship with God's people? ☐ ☐

_____

_____

_____

Total your score: _____

Write the equation: _____

UNIT II

IN THE IMAGE AND LIKENESS OF GOD'S KINGDOM

QUESTION EVALUATION REVIEW

QUESTION EVALUATION REVIEW IN THE IMAGE AND LIKENESS OF GOD'S KINGDOM

MEMORY VERSE

Ephesians 5: 23-25

"For the husband is the head of the wife as Christ is the head of the Church, his body, of which he is the savior. Now as the church submits to Christ, so also wives should submit to their husbands in everything. Husbands, love your wives, just as Christ loved the church and gave himself up for her."

IN THE IMAGE AND LIKENESS OF GOD'S KINGDOM

The exercises listed in this unit are ordered to the questions in unit one Evaluate your Marriage. Review your answers from unit one before commencing completion of each exercise. The following questions in this unit are representing your marriage in the Image and Likeness of God's Kingdom. Use practicality or experience while completing each exercise.

Workshop Two

EXERCISE # 1

REVIEW QUESTION # 6 ☰ DOES THE FACT THAT JESUS CHRIST IS LORD MANIFESTS ITSELF IN PRACTICAL WAYS IN YOUR MARRIAGE?

John 15:5

"I am the vine, ye are the branches: He that abideth in me, and I in him, the same bringeth forth much fruit: for without me ye can do nothing."
KJV

I am the vine; you are the branches. If a man remains in me and I in him, he will bear much fruit; apart from me you can do nothing." NIV

When we abide in Christ by living in Him in obedience to His will, the manifestation of Christ in practical ways will be inevitable. In addition, God living in us bears much fruit. Bearing fruit is the manifestation of the true and living God in us. If you are bearing much fruit, it has to be by the power of the Holy Spirit bearing fruits of the Spirit and obedience to His will in the whole counsel of God, Ga. 5:22. Christ Jesus as the vine is where all the nutrients and vitamins are for the growth of the branches to produce fruit. The sap runs deep, from the roots springing up into the branches where they are beautiful, alive, and thriving to bear fruit. Much fruit comes from fruit you already have after God has pruned you to be even more fruitful, Jo. 15:2. Apart from the vine, you will not be able to survive. There will not be any nutrients or vitamins for you to live on and to live in the vine. Moreover, they will be withered, cut off and thrown into the fire to burn, Jo. 15:6. A dead branch just takes up space and serves no purpose in the life of the vine. The vine gives the life that sustains you, giving you vitality. **Where are you today spiritually in the Lord? Can you truly say you are bearing much fruit? How much are you bearing in your marriage?**

Check the box ☑after you have read and prayed in the power of the Holy Spirit seeking God's understanding where you are Spiritually connected in relationship to him.
❐ Now, remember what the Lord Jesus said to His disciples in Jo. 15: 3. They already had something in them to produce fruit because Jesus had chosen them and cleansed them through His Word. God's Word takes precedence in our minds also when we submit to Him and He takes the initiative to produce something in us. What is that something he produces? Is it not Faith! Faith comes by hearing the Word of God, Ro. 10: 17. In addition, God purified and cleansed our hearts by faith, Ac. 15:9, without physical works. Therefore, the fact is you believed in Jesus, and believing is producing fruit from the vine. Why, sap that runs deep from the roots springing up to the branches is how we bear fruit. (The sap is faith and the Holy Spirit, God gave these as a gift by his grace, Acts 15:9-10.) Yet we do not bear fruit by our own power. The whole idea is to bear much fruit by allowing God to prune what is already there that He initially gave you, faith! Faith producing fruit is everything to those that believe and that are obedient enough to receive it. Believing is a work, and it works, Jo. 6:28-29. For that reason, exercise it in the Lord, in the vine where the sap runs deep. Bearing fruit is the manifestation of Christ Jesus in us.

Here are two examples of faith in marriage. If you agree with the examples, check the boxes ☑ and take the time to pray, looking for practical ways of Christ's manifestation in your marriage.

☐I have faith to produce kindness to my spouse consistently. I help around the house without complaining about it. I do it cheerfully because I love to serve. Is this the right attitude to have in loving kindness to your mate? Check the box ☑ if you agree.

☐I have faith to suffer through bad situations with my spouse consistently. I know they are doing what they can to find a job. I love them so much. I have to trust and believe that God will work through them to continue to have faith and not give up in obedience to His will. Is this the right attitude to have in when suffering bad situations with your mate? Check the box ☑ if you agree.

List some practical ways Christ is manifesting Himself in you and in your marriage presently?

_____

_____

_____

One way Christ is manifesting Himself in you is through your obedience to God's Word, His will, and obeying His commandments.

What are some commandments you are obeying in your marriage? Give some examples!

_____

_____

_____

In what ways is this exercise helpful to your marriage? Moreover, how will you teach others?

_____

_____

_____

EXERCISE # 2

REVIEW QUESTION # 6 📖 DO YOU USE THE BIBLE TO DETERMINE YOUR CONVICTIONS, DECISIONS AND PRACTICES IN LIFE IN GENERAL AND MARRIAGE IN PARTICULAR?

II Cor. 4:2

"But have renounced the hidden things of dishonesty [shame], not walking in craftiness, nor handling the word of God deceitfully; but by manifestation of the truth commending ourselves to every man's conscience in the sight of God." KJV

The manifestation of the truth is the manifestation of Jesus Christ commending us to every man's conscience in the sight of God. Jesus Christ is the Word of God, and studying the Word of God brings us into a deeper relationship with Christ. We cannot separate the truth, the Word of God from Christ Jesus; in the beginning was the Word, the Word was with God, and the Word was God, Jo. 1:1

What are some examples of convictions, decisions, and practices in your household and marriage because of the bible?

_____

_____

_____

In addition, the text above has an example of what convictions, decisions, and practices should not be. One is handling the Word of God deceitfully. In addition, the way we walk should be without shame, dishonesty, and wickedness. We should not live and make decisions based upon our own lust. We may not need that big house right now, or a bigger car. We do not need to beat people up (especially our spouses) with the Bible 📖 to make them see our way. What glorifies God should be at the center of our motivation, along with pleasing Jesus Christ.

If there are, any decisions or convictions that are not in line with the will of God, you need to pray right now and seek God's direction and power. *"Seek ye first the Kingdom of God and His righteousness and all these things shall be added unto you." Matt. 6:33, KJV.* If you are struggling with something that needs God's attention, devote yourself to God right now. Seek God's direction and peace that He is in control of your situation. ☐ **[If you have completed your devotion check the box ☑ and go to the next question review.]**

EXERCISE # 3

REVIEW QUESTION # 3 📖 DO YOU AND YOUR SPOUSE STUDY THE BIBLE, PRAY, WORSHIP GOD, AND SEEK TO SERVE GOD TOGETHER?

Let us look at some passages of Scripture together and draw from them God's will for your marriage and household to study, pray and worship the Lord together. After reading each Scripture, write down what each passage means to you in your marriage and household.

Ephesians 5:25-27

"Husbands, love your wives, just as Christ loved the church and gave himself up for her to make her holy, cleansing her by the washing with water through the word, and to present her to himself as a radiant church, without stain or wrinkle or any other blemish, but holy and blameless." NIV

_____

_____

_____

Matthew 6:33

"But seek first his Kingdom and his righteousness, and all these things will be given to you as well." NIV

_____

_____

_____

Joshua 24:15

"And if it seem evil unto you to serve the Lord, choose you this day whom ye will serve; whether the gods which your fathers served that were on the other side of the flood [were beyond the River], or the gods of the Amorites, in whose land ye dwell but as for me and my house, we will serve the Lord." KJV

John 4: 21-24

"Jesus declared, 'Believe me, woman, a time is coming when you will worship the Father neither on this mountain nor in Jerusalem. You Samaritans worship what you do not know; we worship what we do know, for salvation is from the Jews. Yet a time is coming and has now come when the true worshipers will worship the Father in spirit and truth, for they are the kind of worshipers the Father seeks.'" NIV

The husband's responsibility to the wife is the same as Christ's to the Church. This is a form of the Christ-Church relationship and the Church-Christ relationship. What does this relationship look like along with its image? It is the image and likeness of God's Kingdom in the home and in marriage. Husbands ought to be opening God's Word to his wife and teaching her the truth, and that will do what? Cleanse her with the word, presenting her without spot or wrinkle only through the shed blood of Jesus Christ. The power is not in the man but in Christ Jesus! (Review exercise #1.) We went over what is cleansing by the word. Make no mistake about it; Jesus Christ has already cleansed us through the shedding of His blood through our confession and repentance by the hearing of the word. Husbands, by continuing in the word cleansing, are unflagging. Cleansing is ongoing as we confess and have a penitent heart. In addition, we ought to be seeking first the Kingdom of God and His righteousness and making worship a priority in our homes. Why, God seeks those who worship him not only on Sundays in a building, but worship is daily. Worship is not on mountaintops in special cities or places, it is in our hearts. We take it with us wherever we go. Hence, worship is not something we just do or a thing, it is in the Spirit that lives in us. The Holy Spirit is who leads us to worship. It is a way of life worshiping in spirit and in truth that is a spiritual person. Therefore, Worship is a personal relationship with God and Jesus Christ through the Holy Spirit.

In what ways does this exercise help you to see the importance of worship in your home?

_____

_____

_____

Ψ

EXERCISE # 4

REVIEW QUESTION # 4 📖 DO YOU AND YOUR SPOUSE SEEKS TO PLEASE ONE ANOTHER?

This will come by forming habits of seeking to please each other. For example, the word 'mind' in the greatest commandment, Matt. 22: 37-39, in the original text is the 'faculty'. The word is **dianŏia** 'mind', or the **dianŏia** 'the faculty', deep thought or by implication, its exercise. This is any **natural** endowment or **acquired** power: the faculty of seeing, feeling, reasoning. This is the entire mind or function of the whole mind. In other words, one of the most powerful attributes of the mind is forming habits. The total extent of space develops habits in your mind. As an example, riding a bike or eating your meal with a fork or spoon. You trained your mind to believe this is the right way of doing things. Then it became natural to you without even thinking about it. I call these habitual practices – forming habits of the mind. In the same way, we love ourselves by habitual practices that take care of our needs. Yet, even more so, we can develop loving in a supernatural sense instead of a natural sense. Taking care of ourselves is in the natural, but doing things in the spirit takes new birth, a new self, and a supernatural being **(being led by the Spirit is in the indwelling of the Holy Spirit, Acts 2:38)**. When we love our neighbors as we love ourselves, it is a natural thing to love ourselves from the faculty mind. However, loving within the framework of God takes the supernatural (living in and under the power of the Holy Spirit) because you will love unconditionally, seeking to please one another. Why, in the natural sense, we cannot love consistently and unconditionally. We can during the times we feel like loving. God's love is not a feeling. We seek to please God (in obedience and to glorify Him) with the faculty mind or the **dianŏia**. God is love (agape), I Jo. 4:16, and without God we cannot possibly love. Make no mistake about it; this is why we must form habits to love God. Loving God first will in turn flow outwardly to our spouses, brothers, and sisters in Christ, seeking to please one another with agape love. Hence, as we **habitually** practice loving God we will **habitually** practice loving our neighbors (spouses, family, saints, relatives, surrounding communities, towns, cities, states, our country and the world), starting at home because they are our first neighbors. Husbands and wives are first neighbors, Gen. 2:24, Eph.5: 31. One of our purposes in life is to **leave our father and mother and cleave to our mates.** What is **habitually,** *of pertaining to, or constituting a habit? In other words to result from habit or repeated use. This is something frequently seen and done.*

How do we form habits to love our mates?

_____

_____

_____

We need to be renewed in the spirit of our minds, Eph. 4:23, and be thinking on things that will take precedence in our minds to form habits of change as we act out those things we are thinking. In Ph., 4:8 are things we need to think on, and then we need to train our mind and body working together to practice those spiritual things. Here is an example and after you have committed to forming habits of change, habitual practices, check the box ☑.

❐ Something that is lovely to think and to do is to hug your spouse more often. It is also a commandment! In Romans 16: 16, salute in the KJV and original context of Scripture is in the Greek from the word *aspazŏmai.* This word means *to enfold in the arms, (by implication) to salute, (figurative) to welcome. Welcome is to embrace, greet, and to salute.* Write down how many times you hug your spouse per day in this box ☐.

Now decide to hug your spouse double the amount of times. I challenge you to do this exercise. It will take your relationship to another level. If you hug your mate seldom, start hugging them once per day. You can pick any time of the day you want. However, I challenge you to hug your mate twice per day – when you get up in the morning then once when they come home from work. If you really want to spice it up, add a kiss. ☙ *"Salute one another with a holy kiss. ☙"* You can choose a passionate kiss if you want. However, if you consistently hug and kiss at least once per day, double it to twice per day. If you hug and kiss your spouse twice already, then pump it up to four times a day. If you get off track, continue on the next day. Here is the deal; you have to practice this habitually for thirty days. If you miss a day, you will have to add on a day. At the end of thirty days, you have formed a habit of hugging and kissing your spouse, these are forms of showing love! Love is not a fuzzy feeling, it is a commitment. Committing yourself to changing into a lover, or a greater lover for God towards your mate, will take habitual practice. Hence, they are acts of love. I call this *growing in love. When you grow in love, you will not fall out of love!*

List some other habitual practices, seeking to please your spouse, that you will commit to change?

_____

_____

_____

How will this exercise help you and your mate's relationship?

_____

_____

_____

_____

Y

EXERCISE # 5

REVIEW QUESTION # 12 📄 DO YOU SHOW LOVE IN MANY PRACTICAL AND TANGIBLE WAYS?

With marriage being in the image and likeness of God's Kingdom, we will love to show love in many practical and tangible ways. Why, this is a practice of Matt. 22: 37-39, the greatest commandment and the second like unto it. We learned previously and now know the meaning of loving God, and that is habitual practices of God's Word in obedience to His will! In addition, loving self habitually (by nature) and loving God habitually (supernaturally) is good for oneself. Hence, we love our spouses/neighbors as we love ourselves! In Eph. 5: 28-30 you are inseparable.

Ephesians 5: 28-29

"In this same way, husbands ought to love their wives as their own bodies. He who loves his wife loves himself. After all, no one ever hated his own body, but he feeds and cares for it, just as Christ does the church for we are members of his body." NIV

Ephesians 5: 28-29

"So ought men to love their wives as their own bodies. He that loveth his wife loveth himself. For no man ever yet hated his own flesh; but nourisheth and cherisheth it, even as the Lord [Christ also] the church." KJV

What strikes you the most about these passages and gives some word emphasis between both translations?

Did you notice the words nourish, cherish, care, love, body, and Christ who is the personification of words that are wholesome? He is the word in action, the truth of any word of wholesomeness and a person. If we went back to study each word extensively, including Christ, what would we derive from it, with a new way of thinking?

❐ **Complete a word study on each word listed above. Study Christ as a person (what He did for you) and as God. He personifies words (words of wholesomeness) because He is the Word of God Jo. 1:1. Moreover, He brings words to life! After you have completed the word study, check the box ☑ and write what they mean to you and how you can apply these attributes to your marriage. Remember, make them practical ways you can:**

Nourish your mate– _____

_____

Cherish your mate– _____

_____

Care for your mate– _____

_____

Love your mate– _____

_____

Love your mate's body– _____

_____

See Christ love for you– _____

_____

Here is another exercise for you. In the passage above, it talks about taking care of yourself, especially the man when it comes to the image and likeness of God's Kingdom – Christ loving the Church. However, I am not letting the wives off the hook. God wants both spouses to learn more about one another.

For example, fill in the blanks with these words or phrases. Cool whip with my wife · Golf · Sex · Kissing and touching · Dinner · Lingerie · Whatever food I chose · Board games · Shoes · Kissing toes · Ice cream on my husband's chest · After dinner · After exercising · A rubdown · Pizza · Sporting goods

I like to play_____.

I like to eat_____.

I like to shop for_____.

I like a massage before_____.

I like to slow dance before_____.

I like _____ as foreplay.

I like a rubdown _____.

Here is the deal; incorporate yourself in what your mate likes for themselves. Once you have learned what your mate likes, include yourself and enjoy it! I have given you some practical ways you can fill in the blanks according to your needs or fun time. However, you have no other choices but these alone. Therefore, fill in the blanks with the examples given. Then I challenge you to commence practicing these examples! If you do not like any of these examples, two thumbs down 👎👎, then make up your own selection of words or phrases. Remember, make it fun! 👍👍 ☺

♥ Complete this exercise with what 'your spouse selected' for your involvement with them. After completing this exercise, within seven days write down your experience. Make a note of any change in your perception of showing love in many practical ways, and include your experiences. Make your notes based on the experiences of what you did with your mate and what he or she did with you. Therefore, you have two different exercises to complete. If you need more time, please feel free to take it, there is

**no rush. However, the sooner you start your fun times the better!
Write your experience below.**

_____

_____

_____

_____

_____

_____

_____

_____

_____

_____

_____

_____

_____

SCRIPTURE READING

Song of Songs 8: 1-3

"If only you were to me like a brother who was nursed at my mother's *breasts*! Then, if I found you outside, I would *kiss* you, and no one would despise me. I would lead you and bring you to my mothers' house she who has taught me. I would give you spiced wine to drink, the *nectar* of my *pomegranates*. His left *arm is under my head* and his right *arm embraces me*." NIV

WRITE IN THE COLUMN BELOW

Study the words and phrases in *italic*. What words strike you the most for an intimate moment with your mate? Moreover, why?

EXERCISE # 6

REVIEW QUESTION # 15 📖 DO YOU PRAY FOR ONE ANOTHER, SUPPORT, AND SEEK TO ENCOURAGE ONE ANOTHER?

Make a prayer list for your mate and begin to pray for them daily. What are some areas in their life that are in need of encouragement? What are they struggling with? Be accountable to one another in those areas, it can be sin, trials, etc. On a daily basis, seek to encourage your mate in those areas.

Ephesians 6: 18

"And pray in the Spirit on all occasions with all kinds of prayers and requests. With this in mind, be alert and always keep on praying for all the saints." NIV

Ephesians 6: 18

"Praying always with all prayer and supplication in the Spirit, and watching thereunto with all perseverance and supplication for all saints." KJV

If you notice, all the **key** words are equal in both passages. However, one word may expound more than others but are saying the same thing. Therefore, I would like for us to do another word study, but this time about the importance of praying for one another. I will list the words for you, but you will have to write the meaning of the word next to it as it applies to your prayer life. In addition, pray over each word asking God how to enhance these in your prayer life, by implication, writing your prayer down with dates expecting God to answer them, Mk. 11:24. Remember to pray with forgiveness in your heart, Mk. 24-26. This is the **key** ⤶ to receiving if there is any unforgiveness in the heart. Hence, your spouse is the most important saint in your life!

In the Spirit– _____

_____

_____

All occasions–

_____

_____

All kinds of prayers–

_____

_____

Requests–

_____

_____

With this in mind–

_____

_____

Be alert–

_____

_____

Always keep on praying–

_____

_____

All Saints–

_____

_____

All prayer–

_____

_____

Supplication–

_____

_____

Watching–

_____

_____

What is the proper way to encourage or to support your spouse? Check the appropriate box ☑. If you do not agree with any of the examples, write your reason why.

❐ Only when they encourage will I encourage them.

❐ When I am in the mood to encourage my spouse.

❐ Since I love my mate and care for them at any time of the day or night, I am ready to encourage them.

❐ If my spouse needs encouragement and I am busy, I will tell them to wait until I am finished.

❐ I will drop whatever I am doing and attend to my spouse because I need to support them.

❐ My job is more important to me, so if they call me at work, I will tell them to only call my job if it is an extreme emergency – I am to busy right now.

❐ No matter what I am doing, even if it is my favorite thing I like to do, regardless of whether at work or play, I will stop immediately to attend to my spouse's needs. Why, because they are more important to me then anything else in this world. (With the exception of God.)

❐ Supporting my mate brings me joy because I love them and their well-being means so much to me.

Scripture reading

Philippians 2: 1-4

"If you have any encouragement from being united with Christ, if any comfort from his love, if any fellowship with the Spirit, if any tenderness and compassion, then make my joy complete by being like-minded, having the same love, being one in spirit and purpose. Do nothing out of selfish ambition or vain conceit, but in humility consider others better than yourselves. Each of

> you should look not
> only to your own
> interests, but to the
> interests of others."
> NIV

☐ **What are some prayers requests from your mate? Write them down here and start to pray their behalf – seeking God's direction and power for them. Use the word list to help you pray, and the Spirit will do the rest. He loves working through and by the power of God's Word! If you have made out your prayer lists, check the box ☑ and continue on to the next exercise.**

_____

_____

_____

_____

_____

Ψ

EXERCISE # 7

REVIEW QUESTION # 26 ▤ DO YOU REALLY RESPECT YOUR SPOUSE?

*This is a two-sided question. **First**, it is asking you about your purity in marriage. **Second,** it is asking you about the image and likeness of God's Kingdom in your marriage. Purity and the image and likeness of God's Kingdom go hand in hand. Why, God's Kingdom is holy. He declared it so! To be holy as I am holy, Lev. 20:7.*
Respecting your spouse should start with the fact that they are pure, holy, a wonderful and precious spiritual being created in Christ Jesus. The husband and the wife are no longer in the flesh but in the spirit, Gen. 2:25. Ro. 8:9. After you see each other in this pure and holy state of being, seeing each other in Eph. 5:22-33 is delightful. The fact that the husband respects his wife to love her as Christ loves the Church, the wife sees that she respected by her husband will reverence him, Eph. 5: 33. Marriage is the image and likeness of God's Kingdom and

Church – an institution of holiness. Respect should not come from the flesh but from being in the Spirit. God sees us in a spiritual state of being whose sins He covered by the blood of Jesus Christ, our Lord and Savior, Ro. 8:9, Ro. 4:7. We need to train our minds to see each other in our spiritual state of being as pure and holy, not in the flesh.

♀ *Husbands*

A husband should respect his wife because she represents God's Kingdom, holy and set apart. He is to love her as his own body, Eph. 5:25. A husband loves his own body and takes care of it. Hence, he loves his wife as he loves his own body as he cares for her. In addition, our parents taught us to form habits of love for ourselves as a child and to care for ourselves. Similarly, we form habits of love for our wives, taking care of them in every aspect. Therefore, we will honor our wives, build them up as we cherish and nourish our own bodies. We will care about what they do and encourage them. He respects her because as Christ presents the Church as holy by the washing of the Word of God, a husband presents his wife as holy similarly. In a like manner, husbands ought to be teaching their wives God's Word as God does the cleansing. Teaching, loving, caring, cherishing, and nourishing his wife is similar to what Christ does with the Church. *Why, "present her to him as radiant, without stain or wrinkle, holy and blameless".*

Husbands, list some way's Christ takes care and loves the Church, Eph. 5:25-27.

_____

_____

_____

This is how you respect your wife because of who she is and whom she belongs to. She is a believer and she belongs to Christ Jesus our Lord, a child of God. She represents the church. In addition, respect your wife by praying for her as well. **Read I Pe. 3:7.**

❒ *Husbands, in the same way be considerate as you live with your wives, and treat them with respect as the weaker partner, as heirs with you of the gracious gift of life so that nothing will hinder your prayers, NIV.* **The KJV uses honor in the place of respect. It says to** "give honor unto the wife as unto the weaker vessel". Honor – *timē* is the Greek word *meaning a value or valuables*. An analogy is esteem (especially of the highest degree) or dignity itself. Weaker vessel is *asthĕnēs* in the Greek. This word means strength-less – more feeble, impotent without strength. *Asthĕnēs* comes from the word *sthĕnŏō,* meaning bodily vigor, to strengthen. In the figurative sense to confirm in spiritual knowledge and power. Husbands are to honor their wife to the highest degree, knowing she is in a physical state of being weaker. Moreover, in her spiritual state of being, confirm her spiritually in knowledge and power. Hence, "husbands lead her spiritually", or "to strengthen her and confirm her spiritually". In the same passage, it also says *"to honor or respect your wife as heirs with you or together of the grace of life that is a gracious gift".* Meaning we are equal in having the same promise – salvation. While covered in the lamb's blood, having forgiveness of sins washed and cleansed, no one is greater than the other is. We are equal partners in Christ Jesus. Yet we have different duties and still of the same to submit and serve one another. The husband's duty has a greater responsibility than the wife does. Why, he is to love his wife *as Christ loves the Church*, giving himself for her, Eph. 5:25. Moreover, now the husband can pray for his wife because of his respect for her in the relationship and in Christ Jesus. Therefore, "husbands respect and honor your wife, and pray for her". God said, "Respect is vital so nothing will hinder your prayers."

Check the box ☑ and go to God in prayer, meditating on I Pe. 3:7, afterwards you will have a greater understanding of God's Word. Immersing yourself in this passage is very important while going to God in prayer so that we will truly respect our wives.

Husbands, list how you can respect your wife based on what has been discussed up to this point.

_____

_____

_____

Write down a situation you are dealing with presently that will take honor and respect for your wife in showing love to her – as Christ loves the Church.

_____

_____

_____

⚐ Wives

A wife should respect her husband because of his spiritual state of being first, Gen. 2:25, Ro. 8:9. The wife sees him pure and holy, a spiritual being not in the flesh. After which, you can see them in light of Eph. 5: 22-33. It is a commandment from God to revere your husband in the KJV, and in the NIV to respect him. To revere is from the Greek word **phŏbĕō** – *to frighten, to be alarmed. By analogy to be in awe of, revere, afraid.* In the Webster dictionary revere or reverence means respect. Yet, it is more than that, it is in the light of Christ Jesus and his word. **Read I Pe. 3:6.**

Pray first under God's direction, seeking His understanding in the spirit. Then answer the question and check the box ☑.

❏ **Like Sarah, who obeyed Abraham and called him her master. You are her daughters if you do what is right and do not give way to fear, NIV. Even as Sara obeyed Abraham, calling him lord: whose daughters [children] ye are, as long as ye do well, and are not afraid with any amazement, KJV. Read Gen. 18: 12. Wives, why do you think Sarah called her husband lord?**

_____

_____

Pray first under God's direction, seeking His understanding in the spirit. Then answer the question and check the box ☑.

❏ Sarah was obedient to God by following her husband wherever God sent Abraham. Read Gen. 12: 1-9. Sarah being obedient, in turn she respected her husband. Obedience is respect. Being obedient to God shows respect and reverence for Him. Wives, when you are obedient to God, you will be able to submit to your husband under respect for him. Your husband belongs to Christ and is a Christian. If you listen to your husband, you show respect. If you buck against your husband's (to resist stubbornly or struggle against) duty as the head of the household, I Co. 11: 3, then you are out of order and disrespecting God and the head of your household. How would this behavior disrespect God? To revere your husband is a command, Eph. 5: 33. Maybe your husband is not a Christian or does not obey God's Word. Still, wives you are to submit and to be obedient hence, to respect them, I Pe. 3: 1,2. Why, win over your husband with your spiritual state of being (vs. 3,4), a gentle and quiet spirit, NIV. In the KJV, "a meek and quiet spirit." In addition, in the beatitudes of Christ He said, "Blessed are the meek, for they will inherit the earth," Matt. 5:5. These things are promises from God and to experience in our households. Wives, you will win over your husband by respecting him in gentleness and meekness of spirit. I Pe 3:2 is speaking of a lifestyle of purity (living out your spiritual state of being) or a chaste way of living along with reverence. **Remember this is for the unbelieving husband, how much more is it for the believing husband? Wives in what ways does the church revere Christ? Then in what ways are you to revere your husband?**

_____

_____

_____

_____

_____

_____

Wives, respect your husband also in prayer. Pray for your husband as part of the full armor of God, Eph. 6: 18. What are some ways you can respect or revere your husband in prayer? Make a prayer list if necessary.

_____

_____

_____

� *Husbands and Wives* ♟

In what ways does this exercise enhance your marriage?

_____

_____

_____

⅄

EXERCISE # 8

REVIEW QUESTION # 30 ▤ DO YOU MAKE YOUR RELATIONSHIP WITH YOUR SPOUSE A PRIORITY MATTER?

Ephesians 5: 29-30

"For no man ever yet hated his own flesh; but nourisheth and cherisheth it, even as the Lord the Church: For we are members of His body of his flesh, and of his bones." KJV

♟ *Husbands*

🖝 The Bible said no man ever 'pote', meaning at no time in times past or even once did a man hate his own body. Therefore, if a man or woman shows hatred towards their body, this is because they are in denial. A declaration that a statement is untrue and a contradiction, disowning or disavowal is rejecting oneself, yet you accept it as truth. In addition, it is a refusal to agree with or believe in a doctrine or proposal. They are lost in sin, do not care and do not love God, Matt. 22:37-39. Moreover, we are commanded to love ourselves by nature. It is a natural thing. It is unnatural not to love ourselves. *Love your neighbor as yourself, never ever hate your own body.* People just refuse to love anyone, including God, while in denial to love themselves. There is no reason why we cannot love people as we love ourselves, *"through the power of the Holy Spirit"* loving God! Therefore, since God said we never hated ourselves, we trained from a babe to take care of our bodies, making them a priority. So now we have the **prerequisite**, no one can ever use *(husbands and wives) "I do not even love myself"* as an excuse not to love others. For we are members of his body, of his flesh and of his bones. Christ loves the Church and takes care of the Church. He nourishes feeds and He cherishes the Church more than we can ever do for ourselves. Yet we do the same for ourselves, it is called love.

What are some ways husbands can you nourish and cherish their wife as Christ does the Church?

_____

_____

_____

Husbands, consider not being able to use "I do not even love myself so how can I love my wife?" You take care of your own bodies. You feed it and cherish it as Christ does the Church. How much more is your wife a priority over your own body? Give examples! Review your previous exercises at this time and extract from them to formulate your answer.

_____

_____

_____

_____

What is Christ doing for the Church? Read Ro. 3: 23-24

_____

_____

_____

In spite of our sin, Jesus Christ justified us freely while we deserved our due punishment. Christ Jesus saves me through the redemption that came by His grace. Husbands, in spite of our wives' faults and flaws, we give them grace and love them even if they are guilty. We take on the responsibility of the matter and nail it to the cross. We must be forgiving, while they learn their consequences; husbands are loving, caring, and affectionate through it all. Love them unconditionally and pray for them. Priority, how much will it take? By nature, we make our bodies a priority in life. We have formed habits to nourish and cherish our bodies. These are called habitual practices. We have to learn to habitually love our wives. First, she must be or become our priority in life starting now. It is never too late to start. However, God is first and the last, Alpha and the Omega, Rev. 1:8, 17. Have no other gods before me, Ex. 20:3 therefore, prioritize your wife before any other human being or thing, especially your parents, Gen. 2:24, Eph. 5: 31.

Give an example of a husband in the role of Christ to his wife?

_____

_____

_____

In what ways can you put your wife before anyone else or anything else other than God?

_____

_____

_____

♀ Wives

"And God said, it is not good that the man should be alone; I will make him a helpmeet for him." Gen. 2: 18 KJV.

Let us look at 'helpmeet' from the original context. Help is called **'ezer - ayzer'** the Chaldean and Hebrew word meaning 'aid.' You are your husband's aid.
Let us take this same word, **'ezer or ayzer',** and see help recorded elsewhere in the context of aid in God's Word.

Exodus 18: 4
[God was the aid of Gershon.]
"For the God of my father, said he, was mine help and delivered me from the sword of Pharaoh." KJV

Read Ps. 20:2, 33: 20, 70:5 (ran to David's rescue), 89: 19 (bestowed is help in the original text) Ps 115: 9, 121: 1, and 146: 5. Why did I choose only these passages with the word 'help'? 'Help' in God's Word does not always have the same meaning, yet similar. God used 'aid' in the form of 'rescue' and delivering to assist them in a need. Wives as helpmeet, you are to run to your husband's rescue – that is very significant here. Furthermore, the word also means to protect or succor; from the Hebrew word 'azar - awzar' meaning help rendered in danger, difficulty, or distress, one who or that which affords relief. In addition, the wife is to surround her husband with protection. In modern-day terms, she has got her husband's back! This is the Hebrew, Chaldean translation within the context of Scripture. **Read azar in:**

II Ch. 14:11.
"And Asa cried unto the Lord his God, and said, Lord, it is nothing with [there is none beside] thee to help, whether with many, or with them that have no power [between the mighty and him that hath no strength]: help us, O Lord our God; for we rest on thee, and in thy name we go against this multitude. O Lord, thou art our God; let not man prevail against thee." KJV

"Then Asa called to the Lord his God and said, " Lord, there is no one like you to help the powerless against the mighty. Help us, O Lord our God, for we rely on you, and in your name we have come against this vast army. O Lord, you are our God; do not let man prevail against you." NIV

List some ways you can think of how to be an ezer and an azar.

_____

_____

_____

God has used the wife to bring strength, encouragement and to fill in where needed because of the lack of something in the relationship (read Proverbs 31: 10-31. This proverbs 31 woman fills in where is needed. In verse 11 KJV. *"The heart of her husband doth safely trust in her, so that he shall have no need to spoil [no lack of gain]."* Her husband lacks nothing! She takes care of the home raise the children and a hard worker to help with the income, verses 13, 16-18, 24, and 28. Her husband praises her and the children love her and all she does for the household. She definitely was an *'ezer - ayzer' and a 'azar - awzar' to her husband.*

From verse 11, who is a priority in her life after God? By reviewing the Scriptures from psalms the proverbs 31, a woman, a virtuous woman, delivered her household from hunger and from the need for clothing. They did not have to worry about where the food was coming from, how much it cost, and how it was going to be prepared. Furthermore, she protected them with clothing. She made sure their bodies were covered and secure. She highly esteemed them with her clothing in purple and silk. The colors and fabric represented royalty and wealth. Why, the dye was so expensive. The virtuous woman's family was venerable in the town courts, churches, and schools. Her husband the most important factor here was highly venerable – meriting or commanding veneration because of dignity, nobility, age, or religious or historical associations. He was regarded with respect and deference, verse 23. Wives, are you making your husband look good, feel good, well respected, and venerated among his peers? When a wife makes her husband a priority in her life, everyone will recognize what a good woman and how virtuous you are. It is because of you your husband is venerated, every man desires a virtuous woman. Put your husband first in your life (after God, that makes him actually second next to God) and God will bless you and your marriage! Consequently, your husband is first before anyone else!

How important is the wife to the husband?

_____

_____

_____

> Remember that the husband should lack nothing. What an aid does is fill in where there is a lack, and compliment and share in the plenty. She is a wife of a husband respected and venerated at the gates because of her. She is *virtuous* and of *noble* character!

In what ways can you put your husband before anyone else other than God?

_____

_____

_____

In what ways is your husband venerated within the Church and his peers?
_____

_____

_____

_____

If he is not venerated right now together with the Church and his peers, what are you going to do about it and how?

_____

_____

_____

♀ *Husbands and wives* ♂

How does the Church make Christ look good and venerated with a profound respect and act of worshiping or worship among the world?

_____

_____

_____

In what ways can this exercise enhance your relationship?

_____

_____

_____

Ⴤ

EXERCISE # 9

REVIEW QUESTION # 26 📖 DOES YOU TREAT YOUR MATE WITH RESPECT AND DIGNITY?

Review exercises 7 at this time and then continue to the next question. Does Christ respect the Church? ☐ Yes ☐ No Read Ps. 33: 12-15

"Blessed is the nation who's God is the Lord, the people he chose for his inheritance. From heaven the Lord looks down and sees all mankind; from his dwelling place he watches all who live on earth - he who forms the hearts of all, who considers everything they do." NIV

❐ Consider from the Greek word *bîyn - bene* – to separate mentally (or distinguish) understand, attend, consider, direct, discern, inform, instruct, know, look well to, regard, teach and (cause, make to, get, give, have) understand (ing). Christ respects the Church by considering the Church and separating it from the world. He distinguishes us from the world and understands us. He attends to us, considers us, and He directs us. He informs us, He instructs us, and He knows us. God looks well towards us, regards us, and teaches us. In addition, He causes us, makes us, gets us, gives us, and has us understand or have an understanding of His will. God is serious about our relationship towards Him. From on high He considers us, which is a form of respect for His people. The word respect means – *to have deferential regard for*, meaning we have something that the world does not have. We have a relationship with God *and we have salvation*. In addition, *it is a high regard for and appreciation of worth*, meaning He sent His son to die for us on the cross. Here again, respect means – *to treat with consideration.* Yes, Christ respects His Church in the light of Ps. 33: 12-15. Yet it can only come in the form of God's grace! However, there is a side to respect that we have for Christ not of the same as He has for the Church. This side is a profound respect, meaning to revere to the highest degree! To worship in awe! Look very deeply into the words of Ps. 33: 12-15. Let us look at what He did for His Kingdom. Then, after which, as we represent the image and likeness of God's Kingdom, *we are going to pay close attention to the fact that He considers everything we do, verse 15! (In the KJV it says, he considereth all their works.)*

Now we are going to dissect the meaning of the Hebrew word *bîyn*. I am going to give you each a defined word or phrase to *bîyn*. Then you write down what the word means to your marriage or your relationship. (Give personal application.) *If you understand these exercises, check the box ☑ and continue.*

To separate mentally or distinguish **(Are they set apart in your mind from the world?)**

_____

_____

_____

I understand **(What are the needs and wants I understand about my mate?)**

I attend (What do I attend to to love my mate, and what do I habitually practice at the moment of loving my mate?)

I consider (What do I consider and respect about my mate?)

I direct (What am I contributing in the direction of success in our marriage?)

I discern (What do I discern for our marriage?)

Inform (*I familiarize*) (How are you familiarizing yourself with what you need to know to encourage your mate and to give words of affirmation?)

Instruct (I charge or I command) our marriage too... (*Speak it into existence*)

I know (What do you know about your mate that will draw you closer together?)

_____

_____

_____

I look well to (What can you do to show that you care for your mate's well-being?)

_____

_____

_____

I regard (What do I have regard for in our marriage?)

_____

_____

_____

I teach (I educate, edify, and illuminate) (What blessing can I bring to our relationship?)

_____

_____

_____

I give understanding (What do I want my mate to understand about me?)

_____

_____

_____

In what ways does Christ respect the Church? (Review the above passage of Scripture – Ps. 33:12-15. Pay special attention to verse 15.)

_____

_____

_____

In what ways does the Church respect Christ?

_____

_____

In what ways did your relationship enhance from doing this exercise?

_____

_____

_____

Y

EXERCISE # 10

REVIEW QUESTION # 30 ▤ DO YOU AGREE CONCERNING THE ROLE AND RESPONSIBILITIES OF THE HUSBAND AND WIFE?

Review exercise 7 and 8 at this time to restate your roles in the marriage.

ⵏ _Husbands_

In the beginning, God called the man to be the head of his household. The head of the house is not a figurehead, but one who takes on the full responsibility no matter what. He gave himself for his wife. Who does the husband give himself too? He gives himself to God first and he is to lay his life down for his wife. **Read John 15: 13.**
"Greater love hath no man than this, that a man lay down his life for his friends." KJV
Husbands, are you ready to lay your life down for your wife? I mean literally lay your life down. There is no greater love! Put an open price on your wife. What do I mean by that? If God gave you a check, what would you write on it? If you thought of millions of dollars, that is the wrong thing to do. Let God write out the check for you because He can do more than you could ever imagine or think.
"However, as it is written: no eye has seen, no ear has heard, no mind has conceived what God has prepared for those who love him." I Co. 2:9 NIV.
Value your wife more than anything in this world and give your life for her sake. She deserves your provisions as God provides for us. Ultimately your provision comes from God. Take I Tim. 5:8

very seriously. She will respect you for it. Even though God commanded wives to respect their husband regardless of himself. Read I Peter 3: 1-2. **Nevertheless, there is one other point for the husband.** God called you to be a leader in teaching your household, especially your wife. Gen. 2:16, 17. **(God gave man his law and in turn to give to his helpmeet, his wife). Christ gave the church his word to cleanse it and wash it to make it holy and radiant, Eph. 5:26-29. A man of God loves himself by taking God's Commandments and nourishes his own spirit with God's Word. In turn as Christ teaches the Church as the head, and the head of man. The man teaches his wife as the head of woman like it was in the beginning, I Cor. 11:3. He ought to present his wife radiant in God's Word as he does his own body! Husbands, you have to be in an intimate relationship with God or you will be like Adam, not being obedient to God and His Word. Yet, because of Idolatry Adam had abnegation of what God said. He knew God's Word!**

What do you love about your responsibilities to your relationship with your mate?

Husbands, list some ways that you can lay your life down for your wife.

Wives

Review Proverbs 31, woman a virtuous woman, in exercise 8. Then review the meaning of the helpmeet. Let us highlight some things about the proverbs 31 woman a virtuous woman, and then the helpmeet.

"The heart of her husband doth safely trust in her, so that he shall have no need to spoil [no lack of gain]." Her husband lacks nothing! She takes care of the home, raises the children and is a hard worker to help with the income, verses 13, 16-18, 24, and 28. Her husband praises her and the children love her and all she does for the household. She definitely was a *'ezer - ayzer'* and a *'azar - awzar'* to her husband. Her husband, the most important factor here, was highly venerable – meriting or commanding veneration because of dignity, nobility, age, or religious or historical associations. He was regarded with respect and deference, verse 23. Wives, are you making your husband look good, feel good, well respected, and venerated among his peers? **What strikes you the most about the proverbs 31 woman?**

"And God said, it is not good that the man should be alone; I will make him a helpmeet for him." Gen. 2: 18 KJV.

Let us look at 'helpmeet' from the original context. Help is called **'ezer - ayzer'** the Chaldean and Hebrew word meaning 'aid.' You are your husband's aid.
Let us take this same word, **'ezer or ayzer'**, and see help recorded elsewhere in the context of aid in God's Word. **Exodus 18: 4**, God was the aid of Gershon.

"For the God of my father, said he, was mine help and delivered me from the sword of Pharaoh." KJV

What does ezer mean to you and why?

The word 'help' also mean to protect or succor; from the Hebrew word *'azar - awzar'* meaning help rendered in danger, difficulty, or distress. *One who or that which affords relief. In addition, the wife is to surround her husband with protection. In modern-day terms, she got her husband's back!* **II Ch. 14:11**

*"And Asa cried unto the Lord his God, and said, Lord, it is nothing with [there is none beside] thee to **help**, whether with many, or with them that have no power [between the mighty and him that hath no strength]: **help us**, O Lord our God; for we rest on thee, and in thy*

name we go against this multitude. O Lord, thou art our God; let not man prevail against thee." KJV.

"Then Asa called to the Lord his God and said", Lord, there is no one like you to ***help*** *the powerless against the mighty.* ***Help us****, O Lord our God, for we rely on you, and in your name we have come against this vast army. O Lord, you are our God; do not let man prevail against you." NIV*

Consider Sarah at this point. She protected Abraham by not telling Pharaoh she was Abraham's wife, thinking Abraham would be murdered, Gen. 12: 10-13, Gen. 20:11. She actually had to sleep in another man's quarters to be his wife to save her husband's life, Gen. 12: 15,19! (Pharaoh never lay with her regardless of the law. She belongs to Abraham not Pharaoh. Therefore, God had to step in to preserve Sarah for her husband, Gen. 12: 17). This was a major extreme for Sarah to save her husband's neck. Read Gen 12: 10-19 and Gen. 20: 1-11.

Wives, what strikes you the most about being an azar to your husband according to Sarah?

Husbands and Wives

What is in this exercise that can enhance your roles?

Thought for Today: My Wife as a 'ezer' 'azar'.

Ten years ago, my wife planted a seed in me and gave me a vision. She told me that I was going to be a marital counselor during the time of ministerial struggles. I was an assistant preacher and was not preaching that often. I was searching for God to show me what it was that He wanted me to do in the ministry. I had a strong desire to preach, and I always will. I could not see myself as a marital counselor. My wife was persistent with this ministry. She even started telling people who I was going to be! I kept denying it. However, two weeks later the Holy Spirit became overwhelming. He gave me the largest vision that ever came across my mind. He said that I was to warn the people all over the world that were suffering broken homes and marriages. I was overwhelmed with the vision of taking the gospel of Jesus Christ into the homes of men and women all over the world. God's hand moved me to enroll into biblical counseling weeks later. God is the reason I am helping couples with marriage enrichment because He chose to use my wife in my life! Praise is to God for my wife! She rescued me during the time of struggle while not knowing my full potential of what God called me to be. She planted the seed and encouraged me to be who I am today!

UNIT III

UNDER THE POWER OF HOLY COMMUNICATION IN THE IMAGE AND LIKENESS OF GOD'S KINGDOM

QUESTION EVALUATION REVIEW

QUESTION EVALUATION REVIEW COMMUNICATION IN THE IMAGE AND LIKENESS OF GOD'S KINGDOM

MEMORY VERSE

Ephesians 4: 29

"Do not let any unwholesome talk come out of your mouths, but only what is helpful for building others up according to their needs, that it may benefit those who listen." NIV

UNDER THE POWER OF HOLY COMMUNICATION

In God's Kingdom is the tree of life, Gen. 2:9, Rev. 2:7. Asking for forgiveness breathes life as a part of salvation. Jesus' message assimilates God forgiving us when we forgive others.

EXERCISE # 1

REVIEW QUESTION # 5 📄 DO YOU ASK FOR FORGIVENESS WHEN YOU HAVE DONE SOMETHING WRONG?

Matt. 6: 12, 14, 15.
"Forgive our debts, as we also have forgiven our debtors. For if you forgive men when they sin against you, your heavenly father will also forgive you. But if you do not forgive men their sins, your Father will not forgive your sins." NIV

How do you know if the person forgave you if you do not seek forgiveness from them by asking so they can tell you yes or no? You do not know unless they tell you. I have heard times before when people say I am sorry, the other person never says 'I forgive you'. Forgiveness is a two-way street. There is one person seeking forgiveness, and the other person is doing the forgiving. When the person fails to say 'I forgive you', they have put themselves in a position of God not forgiving them. Forgiveness comes from the heart, and it starts with saying it aloud so the other party can hear you and know they are forgiven. God is the one who ultimately forgives. Yet God commanded us to confess our faults to one another. When we confess our faults, we are seeking forgiveness from our brother or sister number one and two; we may need only prayer and counsel or encouragement. Here is an example of Paul seeking forgiveness because he knows the value of asking, **II Co. 12: 13.**

"How were you inferior to the other churches, except that I was never a burden to you? Forgive me this wrong!" NIV

The whole point here is that Paul saw the importance of wiping his slate clean if he offended anyone. He told the Church at Corinth that he was not in the Kingdom for the money or possessions but for their souls, 12: 14. Paul did this only to make it right and for their relationship with Jesus Christ, 15-19. Paul set it straight that his actions were for their good and not to hurt them in anyway. **While we keep Paul's upright ways in mind by seeking forgiveness, no matter what, let us make a transition here. Consider this passage of Scripture and check ☑ yes/no based on the principle that Jesus is teaching you in reference to seeking forgiveness.**

Matt. 5: 23
"Therefore, if you are offering your gift at the altar and there remember that your brother has something against you, leave your gift there in front of the altar. First go and be reconciled to your brother; then come and offer your gift." NIV

YES/NO	QUESTION:
☐ ☐	Do you believe this person sought just to be sorry?
☐ ☐	Would Jesus teach this principle only to seek being sorry?
☐ ☐	If this person only said 'I am sorry' and there was not an answer from them saying, 'Yes, I forgive you" would they be free from that person?
☐ ☐	If they asks the person to forgive them and they did not give an answer, would they be free from that person?
☐ ☐	What if they ask the person to forgive them and they say no, would they be free from that person?
☐ ☐	Does the person who accepts the forgiveness have to mean it in order for the other party to be free? ☐

Remember that you have to give the person the opportunity to forgive you. In order to have that opportunity, you have to ask for forgiveness? If the person chooses not to forgive you, they are in sin! They are the ones in the position to forgive in order for God to forgive them. The person in the former passage dropped his gift at the altar and went to seek forgiveness so that he would be free from guilt in order to approach God to be free from the sin they have committed! Therefore, they are now set free from guilt and shame in the presence of God for His cleansing as they seek His forgiveness for that particular sin. If the person does not seek forgiveness, they will not, I quote, "be free from guilt and shame in order to be cleansed from the sin they committed." They will be in bondage to that person, and God will not set them free. Why, He will not accept their offering! Their worship to God will only be aperture or in vein. In addition, they will be in bondage to guilt and shame. A shame to seek forgiveness while in guilt. The answers are no, no, no and yes, yes, no.

Now let's use this same principle with this passage of Scripture.

Matt. 18: 15
"If your brother sins against you, go and show him his fault, just between the two of you. If he listens to you, you have won your brother over."

Tell the truth, does it really matter to you to ask will you forgive me?

**The won-over brother asks for forgiveness.
True or False**

**The won-over brother said I am sorry.
True or False**

**Since the Scripture did not tell us that the won-over brother asked for forgiveness. Is the principle, I am sorry or will you forgive me?
I am sorry ☐
Will you forgive Me? ☐**

It is very clear that Jesus wants us to seek forgiveness, not 'I am sorry'. In addition, it is not only up to the person who sinned against their brother or sister in Christ to seek forgiveness. It is also the responsibility of the party sinned against to go and show them their fault. God forbid this process to be taken lightly between both parties. Forgiveness and reconciliation is needed, Jesus' commandments! Wherefore forgiveness is a form of communication that we practice in the Kingdom. Hence, to have holy communication we cannot have any grudges, animosity, or resentment of any kind in our marriage because of 'unforgiveness'! Therefore, let us free ourselves from anything that is holding us back from loving our mates with a deeper passion.

Is there anything, regardless of how small or large holding you back from loving your mate passionately due to 'unforgiveness'? Start writing it here and go and show your mate their fault. Then be reconciled under the power of the Holy Spirit filled with the Love of God!

_____

_____

_____

What are some ways asking for forgiveness can make a difference?

_____

_____

_____

Ⴕ

EXERCISE # 2

REVIEW QUESTION # 8 📖 DO YOU COMMUNICATE WITH ONE ANOTHER ON A DAILY BASIS?

Under the image and likeness of God's Kingdom is communication. Without communication, there is no law or no word from God! In addition, we could not speak to one another without it. The key ↝ communication was originally holy. God created communication and gave it to man, Gen. 2: 26, 3: 8-19. In the beginning, God communicated (spoke into nothingness, timeless darkness in the presence of water) with the words, "Let there be light and it was so," Gen 1: 1,2! God's communication is the reason why we are here by the spoken word, Jo. 1:1-2, Jesus Christ! Therefore, how powerful are words? *"Pro. 18: 21, death and life are in the power of the tongue: and they that love it shall eat the fruit thereof." KJV.* When we communicate, we are speaking either life or death. God speaks life in His communication. He continuously speaks life into our lives by his word and through the power of the Holy Spirit. When we make communication in life habitual, we will eat the fruit thereof, our spoken words. We need to communicate daily and with life!

Which of these spoken words is life and which is death. Write L or D in the appropriate box.

❏ **Hey, baby, did you have a good day today? My day was great.**
❏ **Hey, baby, guess what Mary said today at work, you will never guess. I tell you she is so stupid you will not believe it.**
❏ **Honey, you have to pray for me because nothing is going right.**
❏ **Hey, love, I had a good day, and in spite of the circumstances I had to rebuke them in the name of the Lord because God is so good.**
❏ **Baby, do not be down on your weight, you will lose it. Allow the Holy Spirit to help you. As a matter a fact, I will help you as well. Let us make a goal to lose the weight you want within three to six months.**
❏ **Honey, let us pray about it. God will deliver you from that sin. In The name of Jesus Christ, you are no longer in bondage.**
❏ **God provides according to His will. He already paid the bills with the increase He gave us, so do not worry about them, sweetheart. Let us pray and ask God to direct us and claim it in the name of Jesus to bless us!**

These examples are everyday conversations with so many Christians all over the world. They are very common situations, and God created us to speak life not death. Death came as a result of sin. We have salvation in Christ Jesus! Therefore, let us practice speaking life daily and stop being so negative. Let us look at an example from the Bible.

"Now therefore let it please thee to bless the house of thy servant, that it may be before thee for ever: for thou blesses, O Lord, and it shall be blessed forever." KJV

In the light of this passage in verse 11 David's seed was promised blessings and benefits.
David only spoke what God had already said He was going to do.
David communicated or spoke words of life, not doubt or death. He believed God and spoke it! We need to practice daily in our speech to speak life and believe it.

What are some conversations that can make good and healthy communication speaking life?

_____

_____

_____

Does this exercise shed some light on everyday holy communication we should be speaking? Do you believe in whatever your conversation may be, God has a principle, commandment or promise for it that can enhance speaking life? If so, what are you going to do about it?

_____

_____

_____

I encourage you to practice this exercise for thirty days. Here is the deal, you are to speak life only, not death. The above everyday conversations can help you. You can talk about baseball and speak either life or death. You can either say things that are positive that bring integrity and positive energy, or negative things. I say, "I hate that baseball player", and this is negative energy. If you do not have anything good to say, then be quiet! If you catch yourself being negative, write it down in a journal and let your mate help you to correct your thinking. Remember to pray daily for this exercise to prosper in your life, becoming a habitual practice. When you have completed this exercise, share your experiences with others. [The answers to the exercise are LDDLLL.]

EXERCISE # 3

REVIEW QUESTION # 8 📄 **DO YOU EXPRESS YOUR OPINIONS, IDEAS, PLANS, ASPIRATIONS, FEARS, FEELINGS, LIKES, ETC TO EACH OTHER?**

Communication is under the image and likeness of God and His Kingdom. Proverbs said communication develops a man in wisdom when he listens to advice. In addition, his or her vision is rooted in the law to keep it that brings true happiness and joy. Proverbs 12: 15, 29: 18.

Pr. 12: 15
"The way of a fool seems right to him, but a wise man listens to advice." NIV

Pr. 29: 18
"Where there is no vision, the people perish but he that keepeth the law; happy is he." KJV

Pr.18: 21
"Death and life are in the power of the tongue: and they that love it shall eat the fruit thereof." KJV

Pr. 6: 2-3
"If you have been trapped by what you said, ensnared by the words of your mouth, then do this, my son, to free yourself, since you have fallen into your neighbors hands: Go and humble yourself; press your plea with your neighbor!" NIV

(Remember, your mate is your first neighbor of contact. Review the greatest commandment, Matt. 22: 37-39.) If there are some things that you said that you really meant, but it did not come out right, and it was hurtful or misunderstood. Go! Express your feelings, opinions, ideas etc. in God's love.

Here are some expressions of what husbands and wives say on a daily bases. The expressions filled with holy communication are true, and the expressions filled with the flesh are false. Check the appropriate box ☑ that applies.

Can you communicate with holiness? Write in your own words how you would communicate in holiness and how you can communicate in the flesh.	**Why should your opinion matter because I am the head of this house? What I say goes.** **True ☐ False ☐**
	Baby, will you forgive me for how I said that? It did not come out right. I did not mean to hurt you. This is how I am feeling right now. I am going to try to say it filled with God's love and I hope you will understand. **True ☐ False ☐**
	Honey, do you think this is a good idea? I think this will really help our relationship. **True ☐ False ☐**
	I believe what I said was right, and I do not have to apologize. I do not care how you feel about it. I am right and your way is wrong! **True ☐ False ☐**
	Sweetheart, I am afraid that your idea will not work. Can we sit down, discuss this first, and seek God's direction? **True ☐ False ☐**
	I think that is a stupid idea; that is not going to work. We should do it this way! **True ☐ False ☐**
	Baby, what you expressed is great! Let us pray about it first and then wait on God to give us the best answer. **True ☐ False ☐**
	Baby, let us pray on buying a new car. I am afraid

the car I am driving is not going to last very much longer.
True ☐ False ☐

Honey, I am ready to have a baby! I am not getting any younger. What do you think, sweetheart? I prayed about this thing!
True ☐ False ☐

That is not right to pray about a child and not consider how I feel! You never ask me first! God does not want us to have it!
True ☐ False ☐

Do any of these true and false expressions resemble anything in your life? The expressions do not have to be on cue with your situation. They only need a resemblance what you encountered in a conversation. Therefore, what are some expressions that strike you the most? (Be practical in your comments.)

_____

_____

_____

How do you find this exercise helpful to your marriage? In what ways can this exercise enrich or enhance your marriage?

_____

_____

_____

Answers to the expressions: F T T F T F T T T F

EXERCISE # 4

REVIEW QUESTION #10 📖 DO YOU AND YOUR MATE UNDERSTAND EACH OTHER WHEN YOU TRY TO EXPRESS YOURSELVES?

When you try to understand each other in the flesh, it will not work. In the **beginning** with man and woman they played the blame game. They hid from God, quarreled amongst themselves, and blamed everyone except for themselves. Read Gen. 3: 8-16. (Adam blamed the woman, verse 12, indicating that he had something against his wife for giving him the fruit, and God for giving him the woman.) Wherefore, their quarreling came to light as God brought it out in Scripture so that we would understand something about ourselves when it comes to communication and behavior.

Gen. 3: 16
"To the woman he said, "I will greatly increase your pains in childbearing; with pain you will give birth to children. Your desire will be for your husband, and he will rule over you." NIV (Read Gen. 4: 6)

The desire unto your husband is not to love and to cherish him. In text 3: 16 and 4: 7 is the same exact word in context of Scripture! Let me break it down for you as humbly as I can based on the Word of God. You might find this disturbing to you; however, if you want to understand each other from Scripture, then I suggest you take heed. Desire is from the Hebrew word *teshûwqâh*, meaning from *shûwq* in the original sense stretching out after; a longing: desire from the word *shûwq*, meaning to run after or over, that is to overflow. What does all this mean? Just as sin desires you – and unto thee shall be his desire, KJV – to run after, to run over, and to overflow with a stretching out after, and a longing to run over or overflow in your life. The wife is to the husband! This is the wife's sinful nature! It caused her to have this desire to run after or run over her husband. She has a sinful nature to overflow his life. The meaning states also like running water, like a cup overflowing with water; the wife is subject to her sinful nature in her husband's life. There are times when she acts as if she is the head of the household by wanting the last word or the act of leadership. The decision maker, "I want my way and that is the way it is going to be. I do not trust my husband's decisions." Wives, let your husbands be men and serve the role God has called him to serve. In like manner, Sarah had the last decision in making one of the most costly mistakes in the history of God's Kingdom. **Read Gen. 16**. In the same manner, Eve played into Adam and gave him the fruit to eat, disobeying God. In addition, the men in both historical accounts gave in to these costly mistakes. The bottom line is sin! Nonetheless, the answer to the problem is in the same context of Scripture; number one is…

Gen. 3: 15.
𝄞 "And I will put enmity between thee and the woman, and between thy seed and her seed; it shall bruise thy head, and thou shalt bruise his heel, KJV." In the NIV the Scripture said, "the seed will crush your head (speaking of the devil) and you will strike his heel."
Number two is Gen. 3:16 c.
"And he will rule over you."

This is not an inferior rule; it is only a position, like a governor. Yet there is a higher authority over the governor, the king! Jesus, who is the seed that crushed the devil's head, is the King and whatever he says is what the governor takes heed to. In addition, Jesus did not tell the husband to be dogmatic with his rule or position of leadership in the home! Jesus' rule is full of grace and mercy, peace and longsuffering. The greatest love ever acclaimed to mankind – **Agape love!** This is why as in the image and likeness of God's Kingdom, the man is to love his wife as Christ loves the Church! In addition, the wife is to be subject unto the husband as the Church is to Christ, Eph. 5: 23-25. Consequently, we have the bona fide answer to understanding each other, along with our purity state of being. Before the fall, Adam and Eve did not see each other in the flesh: "that is seeing each other in the flesh are the roots to the problem to begin with". They were not ashamed in there nakedness in the beginning. Nakedness is the state of purity, stripped of all fleshly desires! We are to be naked in the spiritual sense before God! Suddenly to be stripped of shame, guilt, and sin! Man and woman beginning in their nakedness depicts a picture of holiness and purity while in the flesh. Flesh is not evil; it is the result of sin that depicts flesh to be evil. In plain English, the flesh is now our carnal thinking and actions. A direct prerequisite of our sinful behavior! On that account, understanding each other is to see each other in our spiritual state of being as pure and holy, wonderful, precious, spiritual beings. **"God called us not to see each other in the flesh, but in the spirit!"**

Ro. 8: 9
"But ye are not in the flesh, but in the Spirit, if so be that the Spirit of God dwell in you. Now if any man have not the Spirit of Christ, he is none of his." KJV

You have to look beyond the flesh and see each other as wonderful, precious, spiritual beings, pure and holy. What are we to understand about our mates under holy communication? First, let us make sure we are not acting in the flesh in our sinful nature. Wives, do not let the desire unto your husband take precedence. Husbands, make sure your rule or leadership is in the love of God. Second, make sure you understand each other in your spiritual state of being. Thirdly, if your mate says something like this, "You just do not understand me," what should the immediate response be? Let us go to God in prayer! What we say or express may not be in agreement with each other. Therefore, lean on God when you do not understand your mate. Let Him reveal the truth about your mate, what you need to understand. Pray together and wait for a word from God. Accordingly, we need to practice these truths under holy communication to understand each other while expressing ourselves.

What are the truths to understand each other? Check the box ☑ that applies.

Write in your own words what the truths are for understanding each other in holy communication while expressing ourselves.

❐ **Make sure we are not acting in the flesh of our sinful nature.**
❐ **Wives, do not let the desire unto your husband take precedence.**
❐ **Make sure we have control over each other.**
❐ **Husbands, make sure your rule or leadership is in the love of God.**
❐ **Husbands and wives, it is OK to have your own way.**
❐ **Make sure we understand each other in our spiritual state of being, holy and pure.**

Does this exercise help you to understand your mate to enrich your relationship – explain?

_____

_____

_____

Ⴘ

EXERCISE # 5

REVIEW QUESTION # 14 📄 IS YOUR CONVERSATION PLEASANT AND FRIENDLY.

Under the image and likeness of God's Kingdom, communication is the key to our relationships (review exercise #2). We need to communicate with our spouses in purity, Gen. 2:25. They were both naked and not ashamed, their minds were pure! Their conversation was pure before the fall. Remember Romans 8: 9, we are not in the flesh but in spirit. This is how Adam and Eve saw each other! Jesus Christ gave us that capacity to see each other in the spirit. Unfortunately, our flesh gets in the way of our vision. In Ro. 8: 8 it says, *"so then they that are in the flesh cannot please God." KJV.* If we see our spouses in the flesh, we will stand the chance of having pleasant and friendly conversations. Odds will be against us if our conversations get heated. We will easily recourse to the flesh. Job's wife looked at her husband in his fleshly state of being. She did not look at Job in his spiritual state of being. If she had, she would have known that Job was in the hands of God. Her wonderful precious husband was a spiritual minded Jew that trusted in God (meaning he worshiped the one and only true God, Jehovah). However, up until this point in time, in her life and in Job's life, she let circumstance distort her thinking about God and her husband! Job 2: 9. Was this conversation pleasant and friendly? No, it was full of corrupt communication or unwholesome talk. **Read Eph. 4: 29.**

"Do not let any unwholesome talk come out of your mouths, but what is helpful for building others up according to their needs, that it may benefit those who listen, NIV or that it may minister grace unto the hearers." KJV

Describe in your own words what is pleasant.

_____

_____

_____

Describe in your own words what is friendly.

_____

_____

_____

How does pleasant and friendly relate mutually to wholesome, building, benefit, minister, and grace?

_____

_____

_____

Fill in the blank with pleasant and friendly words. Chose words from this category. • Love • hate • stupid • special • wonderful • great job • you dummy • dumb • fool
• good work • you fool • thoughtful • hurtful • lovely • I care • I love you • I do not care • I care for you • my wonderful husband • my precious wife • write in the name of the person • honey • baby • fill in your own words

You did a _____ although it was not exactly, as I wanted it _____.
That was really _____.
I cannot believe you did that, but you are still a _____ person in my life.
What are you doing? That was my food you ate _____ you should have asked first.
I know you did not do that _____. That was _____.
_____ how do you expect me to feel?

It is time to go _____ you are making us late
_____. _____ if you are not finished, but it is
time to go.
What is this _____? This is what you got me for Christmas.
It is _____.
This is my birthday gift _____ it is _____.
I cannot believe you forgot our wedding anniversary
_____. I wanted to do something special on our
anniversary. I _____ you and/but what are you/we going to
do now _____.

Did you identify with these filled in the blanks illustrating Eph. 4:
29? If so, explain.

_____

_____

_____

Did you receive any new ideas from this exercise for your
communication in your marriage? Moreover, how will it help?

_____

_____

_____

Y

EXERCISE # 6

REVIEW QUESTION # 24 📄 DO YOU REFUSE TO LIE TO YOUR
SPOUSE? ARE YOU BUILDING YOUR RELATIONSHIP ON
SPEAKING THE TRUTH?

We are in the likeness and image of God, and God is not a liar!
Subsequently your marriage is in the image and likeness of God's
Kingdom/Church. **How can we lie to each other with these
attributes and characteristics as a believer?** We are believers in
Christ Jesus based on who we are and whom we belong to. We must
tell the truth, it is an inherited characteristic from God. Paul said in
Romans 4: 24, the KJV says God imputed (attributed) righteousness to
us. [The NIV say's God credited righteousness to us.] God attributed

righteousness to us, to be in right standing with Him. God's righteousness fashions our attributes. Furthermore, Christ said it is Satan who is the father of lies, John 8: 44. Make no mistake about it, the Church is not set up to lie but to tell the truth in Christ Jesus!

What are Abraham's consequences for his lies, Gen. 12: 12-13, 20: 2 and are they justifiable?

_____

_____

_____

What are David's consequences for his lie and deceit, II Sam 12: 7-14?

_____

_____

_____

Give some examples of how we can speak the truth to our mates. Have you ever been tempted to lie (include telling the whole truth so help us God!)? How did I help you? Cor. 10: 13. Before answering this question, is there a lie that needs forgiveness? If so, go before God in prayer first, seeking to be filled with the Holy Spirit. [Review exercise # 1]

_____

_____

_____

Does this exercise help you in your relationship with your mate to be cognitive about the importance of speaking the truth? If so, how?

_____

_____

_____

EXERCISE # 7

REVIEW QUESTION # 34 📖 ARE YOU WILLING TO FACE, DISCUSS, AND LOOK FOR SCRIPTURAL SOLUTIONS TO PROBLEMS WITHOUT BLOWING UP OR ATTACKING THE OTHER PERSON?

Review Unit 2 exercise number two (#2). The Holy Spirit acts within the Word of God and His job is to convict of sin, righteousness, and judgment.

Jo. 16: 8-11
"And when he is come, he will reprove [convict] the world of sin, and of righteousness, and of judgment: of sin, because they believe not on me; of judgment, because the prince of this world is judged." KJV

The Holy Spirit will convict us especially as believers. If our decisions, convictions, and practices in life are sinful, the Spirit will convict us of our sin or sins. The Holy Spirit will also convict us of righteousness under the power of Jesus Christ. Paul said in Ro. 4:24, in the KJV that God imputed righteousness, and in the NIV he credited righteousness for us who believe in him who raised Jesus Christ from the dead. If we are having problems in the utmost need of God's help, seek ye first the Kingdom of God and His righteousness! We need to solve all problems God imputed (attributed) righteousness to us. [The NIV says God credited righteousness to us.] God attributed righteousness to us, to be in the right standing with Him. God's righteousness fashions our attributes. Therefore, the Holy Spirit will continue to convict us of righteousness. Daily we are incarcerated to righteousness, all who believe, while we walk in it! Conformably, Jesus had already empowered us too. The Word of God leads us to conviction to do what God commanded by the power of the Holy Spirit! God's Word should always be the solution to the problem. In addition, there is no need to get upset for thus said the Lord! Consequently, I move towards God where he is working in my life, through His Word trusting in Him and obedient to His will. This will lead me not to attack the other person – my wonderful precious mate in Christ Jesus.

Each scenario is either based on the Holy Spirit working through the Word of God in the lives of the husband and wife, or the husband and wife living in the flesh and not the Spirit. Answer each scenario either true of false. True bearing in the Spirit and false bearing in the flesh.

Do you have any ideas? Well go right ahead and write down some of yours.

I have the privilege to blow up when using God's Word to solve our problems.
True ☐ False ☐

I do not want to be wrong, I want to be right, so that keeps me using God's Word to solve our problems.
True ☐ False ☐

As a true believer, it is inevitable while using the Word of God for solutions to our problems that the Holy Spirit will convict me of sin, righteousness, and judgment.
True ☐ False ☐

The Word of God solves all problems in Christ Jesus according to our will.
True ☐ False ☐

The Word of God solves all problems in Christ Jesus according to His will.
True ☐ False ☐

If we just have faith in God and trust in His Word, we will have solutions to our problems.
True ☐ False ☐

The Holy Spirit will force His way into my life when I refuse to listen to His Word and convict me to change.
True ☐ False ☐

If I look for scriptural solutions as a true believer, the Holy Spirit will convict me of

righteousness that will lead me not to attack my mate.
True ☐ False ☐

I do not need God's Word to solve all my problems; I can solve them on my own.
True ☐ False ☐

This is what the Bible says so either you do it my way according to the Bible or we might as well forget about the whole thing!
True ☐ False ☐

Review all the false answers then correct the fleshly thinking into spirit-filled thinking.

_____
_____
_____
_____
_____
_____
_____
_____

[The wrong Answers are 1 4 7 9 10]

In what ways does this exercise focus on how to use scriptural solutions to solve your problems?

_____
_____
_____

THE HOLY COMMUNICATION SCRIPTURE SESSON

I Th. 2: 3, 4, 8

"For the appeal we make does not spring from error or impure motives, nor are we trying to trick you. On the contrary, we speak as men approved by God to be entrusted with the gospel. We are not trying to please men but God, who tests our hearts, NIV. So being affectionately desirous of you, we were willing to have imparted unto you, not the

> gospel of God only, but also our own souls, because ye were dear
> unto us." KJV

What does this passage mean to you and why?

_____

_____

_____

UNIT IV

PURITY IN THE HOME

QUESTION EVALUATION REVIEW

QUESTION EVALUATION REVIEW PURITY IN THE HOME

MEMORY VERSE

Gen. 2:7

"The Lord God formed the man from the dust of the ground and breathed into his nostrils the breath of life, and the man became a living being." NIV

PURITY IN THE HOME

God intended for man and woman to be pure and holy, Gen. 2:25. He created one man for one woman in purity and holiness, period! Believers seeing each other in a different light can be a major problem in our lives. Why, in the beginning when *sin* separated man and woman from God, they no longer operated in holiness but in the flesh outside of God and Christ! This behavior affected the whole world, even today. While, in this state of being, Christ died for us, we believed and He saved us, Ro. 5:8. However, this does not mean we will automatically or by chance start living out who we are in Christ Jesus. Who we are by grace, a wonderful, precious, pure and holy spiritual being. Saved by grace *is who we are*, surrendered and under *total* subjection to the living Christ daily. This kind of living takes practice. It is like qualifying for the Olympic games. Yet *we have already qualified.* While undergoing training in sweat and tears *becoming the total subjected believer we are in Christ Jesus. (Read I Corinthians 9:24-27).* We are already victorious and in a position of righteousness in Christ Jesus, Ro. 4:24.

This unit will teach us how to refocus our minds in changing how we think and see others and ourselves. We will no longer see ourselves in the flesh but in the spirit. The flesh is our shameful and sinful nature. Therefore, we can only live and breathe by the power of God and His Spirit. (Review the memory verse at this time.) God breathed into the nostrils of man the breath of life. This breath (divine inspiration) gave them life and man and woman filled with the Spirit in a perfect relationship to God to live for God in relationship to Him. "They were naked and not ashamed." Indicating that they were pure and holy beings. This is how they viewed themselves as they were! This is how we will see ourselves as God sees us! As reborn again believers in Christ Jesus, pure and holy, period. This view of ourselves will help us to love, respect, and care for one another in the spirit of Christ. Therefore, run the race as if you are running for the prize. We have to beat our bodies under subjection to Christ! Train hard, husbands and wives, and win your prize!

EXERCISE # 1

REVIEW QUESTION # 6 📄 DO YOU ALLOW YOUR MATE TO DISAGREE WITH YOU OR MAKE A MISTAKE WITHOUT BECOMING NASTY OR PUNISHING THEM?

Your marriage is pure through salvation in Jesus Christ. In the beginning, God created man and woman pure and holy. There was no shame among them, Gen. 2:25. Paul said we are no longer in the flesh but in the spirit, Ro. 8: 9-11. Christ living in us replaced the flesh. Why, the flesh is dead and no longer alive in us. Therefore, when we see each other, we see a wonderful, precious, spiritual being alive in Christ Jesus. When we act nastily toward our mate, looking at their mistake or having a disagreement, it is because we are looking at our mate in the flesh, *"the fleshly state of being,"* not in the spirit *"the spiritual state of being"*. We say things that we really do not mean. We become our old man, which is corrupt according to the deceitful lusts, Eph. 4: 22. We deceive ourselves thinking our timetable, plans, agenda, thoughts, actions are better than the other person's interest while in *our fleshly state of being. "Let nothing be done through strife or vain glory; but in lowliness of mind let each esteem other better than themselves. Look not every man on his own things, but every man also on the things of others."* Phi. 2: 3-4 KJV. In the NIV verse 3 says, *"each of you should look not only to your own interests, but also to the interests of others."* On that account, the flesh should not take precedence in our minds but be renewed in the spirit of our mind, Eph. 4: 23. We need to put off the old man and put on the new man, who we are in Christ Jesus. He created us in His righteousness and true holiness, Eph. 4:24, (this is our new birth state of being). I have highlighted the difference between the spiritual state of being and the fleshly state of being. Remember that we are not above the other person, Phi. 2:3. In addition, we have all sinned and come short of the glory of God, Ro. 3:23. Moreover, look at God's Word here in…

II Cor. 3: 5.

"Not that we are sufficient of ourselves to think any thing as of ourselves; but our sufficiency is of God." KJV

Who are we to look at other people's mistakes with a nasty attitude not sufficient or adequate of ourselves? In other words, we should not even think of ourselves as anything other than it is only by God's adequacy and all sufficient power that we can do anything right! We are not right unless it is God's righteousness! Therefore, it is not about us, it is all about God. With that said, what right do we have to get angry or upset with anyone looking at their flesh while we are in the flesh not adequate to think or do anything without God? We have no right and we need to repent.

Let us look at the fact of the matter that we are not adequate or sufficient to think or do anything without God! Which scenario is in the spirit or in the flesh? Check ☑️God's adequacy or ☑️ your adequacy.

| Why don't you give it a shot? Come up with your own scenarios. | I cannot believe you! I do not think that was good.

❏God's adequacy ❏Your adequacy

You are stupid to think that will work.

❏ God's adequacy ❏Your adequacy

You fool, the things you do get on my nerves and I cannot stand you.

❏ God's adequacy ❏Your adequacy

I could have done better than that. I knew your decision was wrong. How can You be a Christian? A Christian would not be like you!

❏ God's adequacy ❏Your |

adequacy

We should have prayed about this decision first to seek His direction and answers through His Word.

☐ God's adequacy ☐ Your adequacy

Do you think this glorifies God? Do you truly believe you are right?

☐ God's adequacy ☐ Your adequacy

I do not agree with you, honey. I will pray and put this in God's hands.

☐ God's adequacy ☐ Your adequacy

Where is God in this? He is going to punish you for your stupid mistakes

☐ God's adequacy ☐ Your adequacy

What does this exercise have to do with how we see each other and ourselves?

_____

_____

_____

If we do not see each other and ourselves as pure and holy spiritual beings, we will act just the opposite. We will only see our adequacy that amounts to nothing, our "fleshly state of being". Rather, it is God's adequacy and our dependencies on Him to live,

think, speak, and walk in this life. Answers: Y, Y, Y, Y, G, G, G, and Y

The other part to these scenarios is that sometimes husbands and wives may punish one another. I cannot stress this enough. When husbands and wives see each other in the spiritual state of being, they will be able to express God's love with passion. I know because I literally trained my mind to see my wife and kids as *wonderful precious spiritual beings*. My love and respect for them progressed to another level. Yet, I still need God's help to live a holy and righteous life. Secondly, my love for my wife and kids is not perfect. I have not arrived. I am still running the race as if I have won the prize. I am becoming who I am in Christ Jesus. The totality of my heart, mind, soul and strength under subjection to Christ is who I am, and who I am becoming in Christ Jesus, Matt. 22:37-39. I have to beat my body and make it my slave day and night to win the prize. On that account, why should I punish my wife? On the contrary, renewing my mind is **"hard-core"** training. My mind has to be in training and challenged to think in the spirit and not in the flesh. One way is to train my mind to look not to my own things (interests) but to the things of others. Therefore, we do not have time to punish one another if we are looking to one another's interests. Secondly, it is how we see each other! *Nonetheless, here are some examples of what we should not do because of how we see each other (in the fleshly state of being).*

WE SHOULD NOT HOLD BACK ON	WHEN YOUR MATE MAKES A MISTAKE OR WHEN YOUR DISAGREE WITH YOUR MATE, HOW DO YOU SEE THEM?

Sex	As stupid
Cooking a good meal	A dummy
Conversation	A nag
Greetings (to salute one another with a holy kiss)	A witch
	Crazy
Affection	A fool
Time spent with each other	Absurd
Serving in many practical ways	Hated
Putting off anger towards one another	Undesirable
Putting off bitterness towards one another	Disaffection
	Divorced!

Now, is this the way to act? Of course not! Do we act like this because of how we see each other and how we see ourselves? Yes, it is! Consequently, how we see ourselves is how we are going to act. Additionally, we are going to treat each other based on how we see each other, and that is a fact of the matter. **Circle the couple that represents the way you see each other.**

How can your mate be any one of these when God sees you differently?

Make no mistake about it; God's love for us surpasses any type of love that the human mind can think of! How God sees us will not be easy seeing ourselves in that light. Alternatively, it is hard to see anyone else in that way. However, God gave us the faculty of our mind to habitually practice God's way of thinking. Only by training can our minds see each other the way God sees us.

THE GODLY WAY OF SEEING OURSELVES AND EACH OTHER

His friends - Jo 15:44

[Trail of faith] more precious than gold - I Pe 1:7

Holy people - Deut 7:6, 14:2

Above all nations - Deut. 7:6, 14:2

Special people - Deut. 7:6

Royal priesthood - I Pe. 2:9

Peculiar people - I Pe 2:9, Deut. 14:2, 26:18, Tit. 2:14

Peculiar treasure - Ex. 19:5, Ps. 135:4

Precious in His sight - Is. 43:4

Honorable - Is. 43:4

His - Is. 43:1

Wearing His name - Is 43:1, 45:4

In the spirit - Ro. 8:9, Gen. 2:7

Fearfully made - Ps. 139:14

Wonderfully made - Ps. 139:14

Our feet are beautiful - Ps.7, Ro. 10:15

Beautify the meek with salvation - Ps. 149:4

Beauty of an old man is his gray hair - Pro. 20:29

Loved - Is 43:4, Jo. 3:16

Saints - Ps. 31:23, 34:9, 50:5, I Cor. 1:2, 14:33, Eph 6:18.

Light of the world - Matt. 5: 14, Pro. 4:18, Ph. 2:15

Salt of the earth - Matt. 5:14

When we have disagreements start seeing each other and ourselves the way God sees us. When we make mistakes, God's view of us is not the same as ours. *"Therefore, stop doing it your way and do it God's way!"* Furthermore, stop punishing yourself and others, especially your mate.

SEARCH THE SCRIPTURES EXERCISE!

I have another view of yourself. Open your bibles and find God seeing you as blameless. Then write down the passages of Scripture below for reference.

_____

_____

_____

Remember that this view of us as a Church, a body of God's people, as married couples, is conditional. You must be a believer and be practicing your faith in Christ Jesus as Lord. Yet if you are not a believer, there is one view that I know how God sees you, and that is loved, Jo, 3:16! *[Receive Christ Jesus as your Lord and savior. Talk to someone you know that is a Christian.]*

Which view do you appreciate the most of how God sees you daily? Explain why?

_____

_____

_____

Start renewing your mind right now on how you view yourself and others. Memorize Ro. 8:9 and your favorite passage above.

How is this exercise going to help enhance your marriage?

_____

_____

_____

EXERCISE # 2

REVIEW QUESTION # 28 📖 DO YOU CONTROL YOURSELF WHEN YOU ARE MOODY SO THAT YOU DO NOT DISRUPT YOUR FAMILY?

Christians are 'overcomers' and 'overcomers' are Christians. Whoever believes in Jesus Christ overcomes the world, I Jo. 5:4. Christians disrupting their families is of the world, and by overcoming the world we have to deal with our internal struggles. There is a false conception that we can overcome sin by overcoming the world. By no means, the only way to overcome sin is by the Word of God that teaches us to put off sin. Putting off sin by the power of the Holy Spirit is how we overcome sin. However, putting off sin is the key to overcoming the world and worldly behaviors! If we have sin of bitterness, wrath, anger, brawling, and evil speaking, put it off. In addition, we put on kindness, tender heartedness, and compassion towards one another, forgiving even as God for Christ's sake forgave us. We subdued the world because Christ conquered sin and death on the cross. If we are moody and disruptive as a result of sin, we can defeat this kind of behavior by putting it off. Afterwards, putting on righteousness and true holiness, Eph. 4:24.

What are some ways of not being disruptive when we are moody?

_____

_____

_____

Sometimes when we are moody, we become faultfinders to please our flesh. When something is not the way we want it to be, we highlight those things or enlarge them in our minds and complain, murmur, be ugly towards one another and disrupt everything around us. Instead, we should approach it in love, peace, and kindness. Concerning that, why do we get moody in the first place? While being moody, we are in the flesh because the focus is on ourselves even if it is a minor irritation. *I,* what pleases me generally, am the focus. Furthermore, the focus is on how *I* feel, think, or see things. Even if *I* am right, how should *I* approach my mate in love and spirit? Simply put, we need to get real with this situation. Sometimes our moods keep us from acting in the spirit of love because we are in the flesh at this point. Therefore, we need to act on what we know and have practiced in God's Word by the renewing of the spirit of our minds, Eph. 4:23 KJV. Let us take practice for instance; this will form habits of change! (I have covered forming habits of change earlier in the book). *Here is the deal.* While you are moody, *renew* your thinking, and *no matter what is going on,* greet and *salute* your mate with a *holy kiss* before you say or do anything ☙. Then proceed on with your day or evening. Remember what *salute* means. Here it is briefly: *to wrap your hands and clamp them around someone.* This meaning is in the Greek, not in the Webster's. In addition, this will help tear down your moodiness to the fulfilling of the Holy Spirit. You are commanding yourself through God's Word to put action into your life, obeying His teaching. You are now approaching your mate in love and affection. Greatly so, this will produce fruit of kindness, gentleness, meekness, longsuffering, patience, and tender-heartedness if you are sincere with saluting one another passionately. Furthermore, any word, reproof, correction, and instruction in righteousness are more appropriate opportunities of acceptance by your mate, This is all under the power of God's love because you are saluting your mate with a holy kiss. Here is no disruption of the family and no one will be moody any longer.

CLEAN UP OUR MINDS BASED ON R0MANS 8:6, EPHESIANS 4: 23

Ro. 8:6

"The mind of sinful man is death, but the mind controlled by the Spirit is life and peace." NIV

Eph. 4:23

"And be renewed in the spirit of your mind." KJV

God's Spirit starts in our minds. The KJV tells us in Eph. 4:23 to be renewed in the spirit of our minds. *Our spiritual state of being is our mindset.* This is how we think to produce holiness in our actions. If our mind is of the spirit, then our actions are going to be by the power of the Holy Spirit! What is the spirit? Let us look it up in the Greek context taken out of the New Testament. Spirit is the word *pnĕuma* in the Greek. *Pnĕuma* means *breath (blast the breath God used in Gen. 2:6).* It also means *breeze, by analogy a spirit (human) the rational soul (comes from our rational thinking) (by implication) vital principal. Moreover, a mental disposition, (our state of mind), and Christ's spirit, the Holy Spirit: - ghost, life, spirit (-ual, -ually) and mind.* Throughout all the New Testament, everywhere 'spirit' is used referring to God's Spirit, *pnĕuma* is the true meaning! Therefore, God's Spirit gives us rational thinking, a vital principle (meaning life), a mental disposition (meaning the mind of the spirit), Christ Spirit, and a spiritual state of being of holiness. On this account, there is no excuse why we cannot change! Given at new birth we received the *pnĕuma.* We have a spiritual state of being that is holy and pure. We have to just give in to the spirit of our minds where He starts the renewing, and God creates in our minds a new person of his righteous and true holiness, Eph. 4:23-24 KJV. In addition, God gave us the faculty of the mind (rational soul and thinking) where habits form! This mind is in the greatest commandment (we covered this mind earlier). We literally take God's Word and habitually practice it to form a habit that becomes spiritually natural – meaning it becomes a part of you. This is how you entertain and exercise your mind on spiritual things from the word *phrŏnēma* and *phrŏnĕō*. These words come from Ro. 8:6, to entertain and exercise your mind on spiritual things. Because of who we are in Christ Jesus, we have the capacity and the power to form habits, exercise, and entertain our minds on spiritual things for change. *Everybody* can change *as believers* in Christ Jesus!

❑ Now we are back to act on what we know in God's Word and have practiced out by the renewing of the spirit of our minds, Eph. 4:23 KJV. What we have just learned must now be put into action. We will start by again forming habits of change by the renewing the spirit of our mind. We are going to do that by entertaining and exercising our minds on spiritual things. The first step is by memory. Secondly, obedience, thereafter practice, and finally meditation on God's Word daily in continuation of obedience and practice. If you are ready to start this exercise, check the box ☑ and continue.

Memorize Ro, 8:6

Be controlled by the spirit. Where does the spirit start? In our rational thinking, our mental disposition. What must we do to be controlled by the spirit? Change our thinking to the way the Holy Spirit thinks! Remember we have his mental disposition – "the spiritual mind". We have the capacity to think like the Holy Spirit as believers! Pick out a subject from the mind of the Holy Sprit in Ph. 4: 8.

"The subject that I chose whatever is noble or of noble character." NIV.

What am I going to practice that is of noble character? *At this point, knowing that I am moody, I have to force myself to change the way I am thinking. I have to want to be empowered by the Holy Spirit to practice God's Word. The Spirit of God is not going to force His way to change our thinking. Therefore, where is my will power to change? Is it in the flesh or in the spirit? It is not in the flesh, we have the capacity and the power to change in the spirit! Our will power should be in the Spirit of God at this point. Still, this is hard work. Make no mistake about it; we will have to work hard at this exercise!* Let us start with Ro. 16:16, this passage of Scripture is of noble character!

One way of meditating on God's Word daily is by living it out in our lives! Why, it is absorbed into our thinking and way of life. In Ro. 16:16 we will experience a way of life that you never experienced before. We should be saluting our mates with a holy kiss at every opportunity given to us. This will form habits that will enhance our marriages to another level.

This is when we should practice Ro. 16:16 in our homes.

When we get up in the morning, we should salute one another with a holy kiss.

True ❏ False ❏ I do not know ❏

When we are moody, we should salute one another with a holy kiss.

True ❏ False ❏ I do not know ❏

When we come home from work, we should salute our mate with a holy kiss.

True ❏ False ❏ I do not know ❏

Before we have a discussion, we should salute one another with a holy kiss.

True ❏ False ❏ I do not know ❏

Before we go to sleep at night, we should salute our mate with a holy kiss.

True ❏ False ❏ I do not know ❏

For no reason at all, we should salute one another with a holy kiss.

True ❏ False ❏ I do not know ❏

What do you think? Write in your own suggestions when we should practice Ro. 16:16.

While practicing Ro. 16:16 in your family unit, you should have less moodiness present. [Answers, they are all true.]

If you disagree with the answers or find it difficult to practice Ro. 16:16 at every opportunity, write down the times you expect it should be practiced.

_____

_____

Give your biblical explanation as to why Ro. 16:16 should be practiced and when you think it should be practiced?

_____

_____

The biblical explanation as to why it should be practiced at every opportunity is two-fold. The first reason is that we are the Church, the holy temple of God, Lk 17: 21, I Cor. 3:16, 6:19, I Cor. 6:16, and it starts in the home. Secondly, Eph. 5:16-17 tells us to make the most of every opportunity in the NIV. In the KJV, the Word of God tells us to redeem the time.

Eph. 5:15-17

"Be careful, then, how you live – not as unwise but as wise, making the most of every opportunity, because the days are evil. Therefore do not be foolish, but understand what the Lord's will is." NIV

In due course, here you have it. God's Word comes to our rescue again to fulfill our understanding of what we must and should be doing to enhance our way of life as a believer in Christ Jesus. We have no excuses at all to produce the things of God in our lives!

Has this exercise helped your relationship, in what ways?

_____

_____

_____

How can you teach others about this new life experience to practice daily?

_____

_____

_____

Y

EXERCISE # 3

REVIEW QUESTION # 29 📖 **DO YOU SEEK TO CHANGE YOUR SPECIFIC HABITS THAT MAY CAUSE DISCOMFORT TO YOUR SPOUSE?**

This exercise will continue with the theme, "now we are back to act on what we know in God's Word and have practiced by the renewing of the spirit of our minds," Eph. 4:23 KJV. The question is do we have habits that we need to break? In plain English, do we have any bad habits that we need to break? Is the answer yes ☐ or no ☐? Check ☑ one. The answer is yes, of course we do! First, we need to seek to change our bad habits. In other words, we need to find out what habits need to be broken! *"But seek first his kingdom and his righteousness, and all these things will be given to you as well." Matt. 6:33 NIV.* Secondly, we need to repent of those habits. Why, the Scripture says to do what is good, and if you do not, you are in sin. *"Anyone, then, who knows the good he ought to do and doesn't do it, sins." Jam. 4:17 NIV.* Thirdly, we need to entertain and exercise our minds (**phrŏnēma** and **phrŏnĕō)** to form habits of change, Ro. 8:6. Mind in the greatest commandment, Matt. 22: 37, is the **dianŏia**. Meaning deep thought, properly the faculty (mind or its disposition). By implication it is exercise – mind and understanding. The **dianŏia** in plain English is where habits are formed. It is any natural endowment or acquired power: the faculty of seeing, feeling, reasoning. The faculty is any special skill or unusual ability – knack. Here you have it, all natural abilities, or unusual abilities that are obviously habitual practices. Habitual practices are anything natural, skills or behaviors, formed by habits regardless of whether bad or good. Loving God must come from the totality of the mind, our faculty mind. It must be habit forming or habitual practices. The **dianŏia, phrŏnēma** and **phrŏnĕō** all work together to make a complete change! Why, we must practice God's Word to love Him to form habits, entertain, and exercise our minds to change, period. Jesus Christ said, "If you love me, you would keep my commandments," Jo. 14:15.

KEEPING HIS COMMANDMENTS TAKES HABITUAL CHANGE!

What are some bad habits you need to change?

_____

_____

_____

❑**Now I am going to list some bad habits, and the ones your mate has a problem with, circle discomfort. In addition, circle the icon that fits your discomfort the most. Before conducting this exercise, let us go to God in prayer so that the Holy Spirit can use us to be truthful. Furthermore, do not let your mate see your answers until you have both prayed together to remove any guilty conscience that may lead to sin.** *(Remember to practice the forgiveness exercise in unit 3 exercise #1.)* **Limit your choices to three (3). Also discuss your answers with your mate to let them know that you are concerned about change. We can still have fun and be serious about change at the same time. Yet it is possible that discomforts may be selfish.** *"Therefore, do not use discomforts to get what you want but be biblical in referencing your discomforts with God's Word without any contradictions."* **If you understand these exercises, check the box ☑ and continue.**

My mate does not take out the trash regular or at all.
 Causes me discomfort.
🌢✳☹☠🎥⚡ 🌧🌩🌂

Use this section to write in your own discomforts.

My mate does not pick up after him or herself.
Causes me discomfort.
🌢✳☹☠🎥⚡ 🌧🌩🌂

My mate will fuss about anything.   **Causes me discomfort.**

Causes me discomfort.
☀☺☹☠⌨✝ ☂☂☂

They always want their way.
Causes me discomfort.
☀☺☹☠⌨✝ ☂☂☂

My mate never does what I ask of them.
Causes me discomfort.
☀☺☹☠⌨✝ ☂☂☂

They always get in their moods.
Causes me discomfort.
☀☺☹☠⌨✝ ☂☂☂

Causes me discomfort.
☀☺☹☠⌨✝ ☂☂☂

They always want to be right.
Causes me discomfort.
☀☺☹☠⌨✝ ☂☂☂

My mate is very bossy.
Causes me discomfort.
☀☺☹☠⌨✝ ☂☂☂

Causes me discomfort.
☀☺☹☠⌨✝ ☂☂☂

My mate is controlling.
Causes me discomfort.
☀☺☹☠⌨✝ ☂☂☂

They do not let me go anywhere.
Causes me discomfort.
☀☺☹☠⌨✝ ☂☂☂

I cannot shop for what I want.
Causes me discomfort.
☀☺☹☠⌨✝ ☂☂☂

Causes me discomfort.
☀☺☹☠⌨✝ ☂☂☂

They will not let me wear what I want.
Causes me discomfort.
☀☺☹☠⌨✝ ☂☂☂

My mate never takes time out with me.

Causes me discomfort.

My mate only wants to have sex when they want to.

Causes me discomfort.

Causes me discomfort.

I never get a home-cooked meal.

Causes me discomfort.

I am not getting enough affection.

Causes me discomfort.

Causes me discomfort.

My mate does not talk to me.

Causes me discomfort.

My mate only talks to me when they feel like it.

Causes me discomfort.

I do not get hugs regularly.

Causes me discomfort.

Causes me discomfort.

Kissing is not a regular part of our relationship.

Causes me discomfort.

I like foreplay and they do not.

Causes me discomfort.

Causes me discomfort.

If there are any larger scale sins that are listed in Eph. 4: 22- 32 and Col. 3: 5-13, there is another exercise for those sins. Discomforts are simply bad habits that the person may not have known about. If they continue knowing the good and not do it, then it becomes sin. The next steps are bad habits or discomforts to put off to put on new habits by practicing *habit-forming changes.*

After conducting the former exercise and going to God in prayer, write your corresponding Scriptures to your discomforts. Then show your answers to your mate.

♂ YOU ARE NOW ENTERING THE DYNAMIC ♂ HABITUAL CHANGE

♦ DYNAMIC ♦ HABITUAL CHANGE

SCRIPTURE READING

Ro. 12: 2

And be not conformed to this world: but be ye transformed by the renewing of your mind, that ye may prove what is that good, and acceptable, and perfect, will of God, KJV.

Being transformed is a dynamic habitual change. Are you up to the challenge? Are you ready to be serious about change in your life? It can start here with your obedience to God, His perfect will!

⛾ Husbands, after accepting your bad habits in love, word and now in deed, complete this form to have dynamic habitual change.

My specific non-biblical habits	Put off bad habits and biblical reference(s) (ex. Eph. 4:22 Gal. 6:9, II The. 3:13, Jam. 4:17, Ph. 2:3-4)	Put on habitual change and biblical reference(s) (ex. Eph. 4:23-24, Col. 3:10-17, Ro. 8:6, Matt. 22:37, Ph. 2:3-4)	My plan to put on habitual change and not to repeat this bad habit and to respond biblically instead (Ga. 6:9-10, Ro. 12:2, Tit. 2:11-12)

♀ Wives, after accepting your bad habits in love, word, and now deed, complete this form to have dynamic habit forming change.

My specific non-biblical habits	Put off bad habits and biblical reference(s) (ex. Eph. 4:22 Gal. 6:9, II The. 3:13, Jam. 4:17, Ph. 2:3-4)	Put on habitual change and biblical reference(s) (ex. Eph. 4:23-24, Col. 3:10-17, Ro. 8:6, Matt. 22:37, Ph. 2:3-4)	My plan to put on habitual change and not to repeat this bad habit and to respond biblically instead (Ga. 6:9-10, Ro. 12:2, Tit. 2:11-12)

Examples

My specific non-biblical habits	Put off bad habits and biblical reference(s) (ex. Eph. 4:22, Gal. 6:9, II The. 3:13, Jam. 4:17, Ph. 2:3-4)	Put on habitual change and biblical reference(s) (ex. Eph. 4:23-24, Col. 3:10-17, Ro. 8:6, Matt. 22:37-39, Ph. 2:3-4)	My plan to put on habitual change and not to repeat this bad habit and to respond biblically instead (Ga. 6:9-10, Ro. 12:2, Tit 2:11-12)
I have not been taking time out with my wife. Now I know, it discomforts her.	I have been looking to my own interests and ambitions. I have been selfish. When I come home, I start doing things that interest me and not my wife. I work too much and I do not give her enough time according to God's will. I need to put off the sin in Ph. 2:3-4.	I will be renewed in the spirit of my mind and love my wife as I love myself In God's righteousness and true holiness. I need to put on Ph. 2:3-4. I need to put on humility, consider her more than me. In addition, God's Word tells me to look to her interests not so caught up in mine. Her interests are more important than mine.	First, seek God, His righteous and repent. Secondly, memorize Ph. 2:3-4. Purposely make every effort to change my thinking by meditation on God's Word, looking to my wife's interests. When I come home from work, I will pay attention to what went on that day in my wife's life. I will plan to date my wife once per week. Moreover, I will pray, share God's Word and ask what is it that she wants by us spending more time together.

My specific non-biblical habits	Put off bad habits and biblical reference(s) (ex. Eph. 4:22 Gal. 6:9, II The. 3:13, Jam. 4:17, Ph. 2:3-4)	Put on habitual change and biblical reference(s) (ex. Eph. 4:23-24, Col. 3:10-17, Ro. 8:6, Matt. 22:37, Ph. 2:3-4)	My plan to put on habitual change and not to repeat this bad habit and to respond biblically instead (Ga. 6:9-10, Ro. 12:2, Tit. 2:11-12)

After completing this exercise, *"dynamic habitual change"*, be serious about your plan of actions and take it to heart. Apply Gal.

6:9-10, II The. 3:13. Additionally, make the most of every opportunity to walk wise, redeeming the time because the days are evil, Eph. 5:15-16. Are you serious about breaking bad habits and putting on a new man with habitual change? God is creating something in us, Eph. 4: 24, *"His righteous and true holiness"*. *Get serious about it and write down your commitment below to practice your plan for "dynamic habitual change". How long are you going to practice your plan?*

Ϋ́

EXERCISE # 4

REVIEW QUESTION # 28 ▤ DO YOU ACCEPT CORRECTIVE CRITICISMS GRACIOUSLY?

Criticism: *the act, or art of criticizing, (to examine and judge as a critic. This is judging anything by some "standard or criterion". Additionally, to judge severely, censure.) Hence, it is a severe or unfavorable judgment and the principle or rules for judging anything.* **Censure:** *condemnation or blame, meaning disapproval. To express disapproval of, meaning condemn.* **(A spiritual censuring is always towards the disapproved actions not the person or your mate.)** Notice as well in the definition of criticism, judging by a standard or criterion, principle or rules! What will that be? God's standard. What is the Kingdom of God's standard, criterion, principle, or rule? *It is God's holy and unadulterated Word, the Holy Bible!* Therefore, to be able to accept corrective criticism (God's standard, criterion, principle, or rule) graciously you have to be in the spirit, called the **pnĕuma. In your own words write down what is pnĕuma.**

(See Exercise 2 for the meaning of pnĕuma)

We need to take our eyes off self and fix our eyes on God and Christ (putting off the old man). At that time, He equips you to flow in the **pnĕuma.** While, renewed in the **pnĕuma of our mind** the Holy Spirit's mental disposition takes over us or starts to control us. We are now full of life flowing in Christ Spirit. Volitionally walking (exercising our will in action in the spirit) in righteousness and true holiness because God creates this mental disposition in us, Eph. 4:23-24.

Eph. 4:23

"And be renewed in the spirit of your mind; And that ye put on the new man, which after God is created in righteousness and true holiness." KJV

As long as you are under the power of the Holy Spirit after a renewed mind, you are free in Christ Jesus to be able to accept corrective criticism at any time in your life. Therefore, this is a *daily* renewing and replenishment of your mind and soul with the flowing of the Holy Spirit. We should always be ready for admonishment in the **pnĕuma.** **Admonishment** is *to warn, to caution against danger or error. It is to scold or reprove gently. We are to exhort, urge one another or give advice.* God's Word stands on this subject of corrective criticism called admonishing.

Ro. 15: 13-14

"Now the God of hope fill you with all joy and peace in believing, that ye may abound in hope, through the power of the Holy Ghost. And I myself also am persuaded of you, brethren, that ye also are full of goodness, filled with all knowledge, able also to admonish one another." KJV

As husbands and wives, we have to practice this extra hard in our homes. I am referring to full of goodness, filled with all knowledge, and to abound in hope. Abound in hope through the power of the Holy Ghost! Why, we have a sinful nature to attack one another, trying to gain control over one another. Instead of admonishing, it becomes an argument. This is where we need to be ready at all times by a constant renewal of the **pnĕuma** of our minds. Therefore, we will be able to admonish one another in the **pnĕuma.**
When do you have the most difficult time receiving admonishment or corrective criticism from your mate?

Let us look at David's life from God's Word of how to accept admonishment graciously. Although our area of admonishment may not be as severe, David took his rebuke graciously. (Read II Samuel 12: 7-13.) If something as serious as murder, deception, adultery, lies, lust, and covetousness, idolatry (Col. 3:5) was in the heart and actions of David for which he was rebuked, how much more should we be able to accept as a little admonishment from our mates? David had some serious problems, yet his heart, convicted and tranquil, wanted to please God once he realized his sin! Are your decisions as sinful as David's were and as serious in nature? (Depending on the nature of sin, some have greater consequences than others.) Why get bent out of shape when our mate corrects us on things that are not near as serious as David's sins or serious in nature? Consequently, most of our corrections are not to make mistakes, like making a wrong turn at the light or not watching the speed limit. Perhaps our corrections are not to forget to pick up a loaf of bread or a gallon of milk. Moreover, we undoubtedly have problems with little things we do or what our spouses do that aggravate us. Those little things may be important to us and we would like to see change in each other. Conversely, our corrections may be more serious than forgetting a loaf of bread, making wrong turns or having imperfections. It could be a major decision for your family. Nonetheless, nothing is more serious than David's sin, unless we committed David's sin. Yet look at David's response to his correction and rebuke, *"I have sinned against the Lord."* It is about our relationship with God first! Our eye has to be on God and not the person delivering the message. It is because of our relationship with God we respond to admonishment and corrective criticism graciously. From the beginning, David has a strong and intimate relationship with God before this fall in his life. This relationship with God kept David, and hidden in his heart, then the Spirit of God convicted him to repent. God's Spirit opened David's heart and restored him back to that relationship he had with God from the beginning, Ps. 51: 1-4, 9-13, I Sam. 17: 45-47. In addition, for us, once we know the good that we ought to do, we should do it because of our relationship with God, or it is sin, Jam. 4:17. Doing the good we ought to do is not only because of our mate, but moreover, it is because of God. Still and all, the Lord wants us to look to other's interest as well as ours, Ph. 2:3-4. God also expects us to have the mind of Christ, Ph. 2:5. This is why God gave us the **pnĕuma** in having a mental disposition of the Holy Spirit, Christ Spirit. Therefore, we are more than capable of accepting admonishment graciously through the power of the Holy Spirit and by a daily renewal of the mind, Eph. 4:23.

Can you accept corrective criticism or admonishment?
Yes☐ No ☐

Is your acceptance as gracious as David's was in II Sam 12: 13? *(A heart open for change.)*
Yes☐ No ☐

Are you experiencing the **pnĕuma** in your mind under the power of the Holy Spirit when accepting admonishment from your mate?
Yes☐ No ☐

Are you ready to renew your mind daily in the Spirit of Christ?
Yes☐ No ☐

You will always remember the strengths of your relationships and treasure them, with God and your mate.
Yes☐ No ☐

The most difficult times that you experienced when your mate admonished you and gave corrective criticism no longer is affective.
Yes☐ No ☐

Are you willing to make every effort to change little imperfections (faults) that can enhance your marriage?
Yes☐ No ☐

If you answered yes to all these questions, you are now free from the bondage of not being able to receive corrective criticism and admonishment from your mate graciously!

If you did not answer the all the questions truthfully or you have one or more no's, you need to seek God's deliverance and power to put off those things you are holding back.

First, identify what the problems are. (Review your answer to the former question after the Scripture Ro. 15: 13-14.)

Secondly, seek God's deliverance and power in prayer and His Word.

Thirdly, use the worksheet provided in this unit to put off your old self and put on the new self.

Fourthly, after you have been delivered, change all your no's to yeses and be free in Christ Jesus. In addition, start saying yes to the spirit in continuance with your new freedom in Christ Jesus!

What have you learned from this exercise and how will it enhance your marriage?

_____

_____

_____

Are you willing to teach others this new breakthrough? (Explain)

_____

_____

_____

SCRIPTURE READING

Col. 3:3-4

"For you died, and your life is now hidden with Christ in God. When Christ, who is your life, appears, then you also will appear with him in glory."

UNIT V

BUILDING GOD'S KINGDOM TO SUBDUE AND HAVE DOMINION OVER THE EARTH

QUESTION EVALUATION REVIEW

QUESTION EVALUATION REVIEW BUILDING GOD'S KINGDOM TO SUBDUE AND HAVE DOMINION OVER THE EARTH

MEMORY VERSE

Eph. 2: 6

"And God raised us up with Christ and seated us with him in the heavenly realms in Christ Jesus." NIV

BUILDING GOD'S KINGDOM TO SUBDUE AND HAVE DOMINION OVER THE EARTH

In this unit, we will cover areas from the evaluation that may not have an appearance of subduing and having dominion. As what was asked in the introduction to this unit, what are we doing to advance the Kingdom with our money and time? Are we experiencing God in our marriages and teaching it in our communities, and showing the world what God's Kingdom looks like in our homes and marriages? God said to multiply, build families, subdue, and have dominion over the earth. This subject may not seem as if it should be part of any marriage enrichment. Subduing and having dominion is the most important part of this enrichment workshop. Why is it the most important, because we reign in Christ and with Christ Jesus that is our position in Him! Remember our memory verse and take it to heart to practice in our everyday lives. God seated us with Christ and in Christ in the heavenly realms. This is our spiritual position, Eph. 2:6, Rm. 5:17. If we want to defeat Satan and his disciples, it is a spiritual battle, Eph. 6 10 18. Additionally, we are in a spiritual war. Moreover, we are the victors, I Cor. 15:54-58, I Jo.5: 4! Christ Jesus won the war for us, Jo. 16:33! **Therefore, all we have to do is walk in the victory. Why, we subdue to have dominion! As married people in Christ Jesus, we need to be teaching people about Christ and how great God's Kingdom is in marriage and be excited about it, experiencing it! Our marriages are victorious in Christ Jesus! For that reason, let us read Matt. 11: 12.**

Matt. 11: 12

"From the days of John, the Baptist until now, the kingdom of heaven has been forcefully, advancing, and forceful men lay hold of it." NIV

"And from the days of John the Baptist until now the kingdom of heaven suffereth violence, and the violent take it by force." KJV

The key to these passages is the now. We are still under the subduing and dominion age in the Kingdom of God! In the battle of spiritual warfare, we are the victors that take our position in the land by force. The world must know and will know God's Kingdom forcefully advancing without hesitation or doubt but in power and in might! We as **married** people must **lead** the way *in the Kingdom God*. God has always set up his people from the family stance to serve and worship Him in victory. In other words, God's Kingdom starts with every man and woman in their respective homes. Where we live is where we function. How we live on a day-to-day basis is how we are going to function in God's Kingdom! We need to be equipped spiritually, mentally, physically, and financially. Let us go forth with this passage of Scripture in mind while under direct commandment from God to subdue and have dominion over the earth, Gen. 1:28. I have Scriptures in this chapter to help us put off our old thinking and way of life to renew the **pněuma** of our minds. Then we can put on the new man created by God in His righteousness and true holiness, Eph. 4:22-24.

EXERCISE # 1

REVIEW QUESTION # 20 📄 DO YOU AGREE ABOUT HOW YOU SHOULD SPEND MONEY?

How can we subdue and have dominion over our money? When we talk about building God's Kingdom to subdue and have dominion, it starts in the home. One way is by using our money to glorify God. First of all, God said whoever does not take care of his relatives or his own especially that in his household has denied the faith and is worse than an unbeliever, I Tim. 5:8. Spending money is a hot topic especially, apart from tithes and offerings. Why, tithes and offerings are giving back to the Lord, and it is the first fruits of our labor. *Hence, a tithe comes off the top of your income before any spending, Mal 3:8-10, Pr. 3:9-10!* Either you are tithing or you are not. We should not have to agree on giving because giving or tithing is a commandment from God! There is no middle ground. However, when it comes to spending our money, we can get a little carried away with what we actually need or want. Our needs come first in our spending, then our wants after everything is taken care of, including tithes and offerings!

For that reason what is the first step to agreeing on how you should spend money? (Remember. tithes and offerings are not included in this question because it is off the top. No agreements are necessary!)

_____

_____

_____

Was your answer?

A   Going out on Friday nights.

B   Splurging your money.

C   Meeting your wants.

D   Taking care of your household needs.

Our household has to be an example in our community around us. When we meet our household's needs, we are stress free from our necessities. Our home is more at peace when we totally depend on God to provide for us. In addition, doing our share of things that are obedient to God always honors Him. When we are good stewards, taking care of our basic needs, we will be happier people. Jesus said why worry about what we should eat drink or wear? Matt.31-32. In other words, God will provide all that we need! All needs met through Christ Jesus are for us to subdue and have dominion over our homes; we must be at peace, filled with the joy of the Lord. This is one reason why he said to *"seek ye first the kingdom of God, and all his righteous; and all these things shall be added unto you." Matt. 6:33 KJV.* In His Kingdom, seated with Him and in Him in heavenly places is our position in Him, ruling and reigning on this earth in victory in Christ Jesus! Therefore, why worry about our needs? **Consequently, what are our needs? What are your needs for your household?**

_____

_____

_____

[The above answer is D]

All of our needs are different from others, here are some examples listed. Circle your needs that you believe God is ready to fill without worry or doubt.

Needs to be met by God	Why should God meet this need?
Grocery cart	
Basic household bills	
Rent or Mortgage	
A new car	
A new home	
A new job	
A new baby	
A night out on the town	
A dinner and a movie	
A ride in a limo	
A vacation to Mexico	
A vacation to the Caribbean	
A new wardrobe	
A new pair of shoes	

A new motorcycle

A new hairstyle

Get my hair done

Get my hair cut

Add a need:

Discuss: should God meet these needs and are they lined up with His will? Are they wants to consume upon your lust, Jam. 4:3? Are they legitimate needs?

_____

_____

_____

Who does the money belong to when it comes into our homes?

A   The person who brought home the check

B   The person who cashed the check

C   The person who spends the money

D   Whoever's name the bank account is in

E   It is all God's money

Who made up this saying, "this is my money, and this is your money, my account and your account?" Why do couples divide their money from one another to pay bills? **Did God make up this rule or did**

man? Does this type of belief system cause division in the home and why?

_____

_____

_____

> God has always called the household to be responsible for its wealth as one. What do these passages of Scriptures have to say about money in the home as one income?

_Pr. 31:27_

"She looketh well to the ways of her household, and eateth not the bread of idleness." KJV

_____

_____

_____

_Pr. 31: 11-12_

"The heart of her husband doth safely trust in her, so that he shall have no need of spoil [no lack of gain]. She will do him good and not evil all the days of her life." KJV

_____

_____

_____

I Tim. 5:8

"But if any provide not for his own, and especially for those of his own house, he hath denied the faith, and is worse than an infidel [unbeliever]." KJV

_____

_____

_____

The key in every passage is the unity of purpose and ***household, or house is the unity of purpose***. Moreover, in the second passage, the virtuous woman's husband doth safely trust in her, and she will do him good and not evil all the days of her life. The **household** under the Old Testament meaning in the Hebrew is *family, steward, or even temple*. In the Greek 'house' means *domestic or household*. Household is *oneness in the unity of Christ Jesus our Lord*. Why, our homes are the temple as well as our bodies and the Church. **Read Eph. 5:22-33**. Therefore, we need to be willing to see things God's way for our homes to agree. **In addition, God will take care of our wants that are in the will of God.**

Matt. 11: 24

"Therefore I say unto you, what things so ever ye desire, when ye pray, believe that ye receive them, and ye shall have them." KJV

Jam. 4: 15

"For that ye ought to say, if the Lord will, we shall live, and do this, or that."

Ps. 37: 4

Subdue and Have Dominion Over The Earth

"Delight thyself also in the Lord; and he shall give thee the desires of thine heart."

Christ Jesus already knew that we were going to pray according to His will because of what was already written in Psalms. **Delight** in the original text means to soften or make pliable from the Hebrew word ***'ânag***. To soften or make pliable is another saying according to His will. **Pliable,** *bend, twist, easily or to be flexible. In addition, be easily persuaded or controlled!* From the list of needs are some wants as well. We have to agree on what are our wants and are we bending ourselves or being flexible to the will of God? Let us be easily controlled by the Spirit of God and persuaded to do His will in obedience to His commandments. Therefore, we must ask and believe that God will give to us what we desire. **To practice this new agreement in the Lord to give us the desire of our hearts, list below** some of your desires that you want God to fulfill. Use God's Word to determine His will for your desires. (The Scriptures above are for the basis of your decisions.)

The desires of my heart	What is God's will for my desire

After you have written down all your desires and what is God's will for your desires, believe what you have written before the Lord and do not doubt, Jam. 1:6-8. On that account, start praying together for your needs and wants in the Spirit of God. *This exercise should help you and your mate to agree on how to spend money.*

In what ways is this exercise helpful to your marriage, understanding the importance of knowing what your needs and wants are?

_____

_____

_____

Once you determine your needs and wants, that will make it much easier to come together and agree on how to spend money.

EXERCISE # 2

REVIEW QUESTION # 21 📄 DO YOU THINK YOUR SPOUSE IS AS CONCERNED ABOUT YOUR VIEWS ON MONEY AS YOU ARE?

When it comes to subduing and having dominion over the earth, building God's Kingdom has a lot to do with money in many ways. Let us look at Matt. 25: 14-30. First of all, what is a talent? Here is the biblical (historical) definition or historical account of the talent. It was an ancient weight and money unit, equivalent in Palestine to 3,000 shekels. The silver talent was worth upward of $1,000. In addition, God gave this talent according to the servant's ability. **What does the word 'ability' mean to you?**

_____

_____

_____

Here is the biblical account from the Greek. In the context of Scripture 'ability' is from the Greek word **dunamis** and from **dunamai** – _to be able or possible, be of power_. The word **dunamis** means _force_ (subdue) _miraculous power (usually by implication a miracle itself). It is ability, abundance – meaning, might, mightily, mighty deed, (worker or) miracle, power, strength, violence, mighty (wonderful) work._ In addition, this is where we get our English word dynamite. **Duna-** is the root for English words like dynamic, dynamo, dynamite, etc... Jesus said he gave according to the servant's **dunamis**. On that account, God gave, "the master gave", according to how much the servants can **subdue or blow up!** The servant's ability by miracle, mighty deeds, power, strength, as serious as violence, mighty wonder, work in abundance. The servants are taking dominion with the master's money! They are subduing with the money in mighty works! Look how serious God is about money, even to the point of violence. Note here that God is not talking about physical violence; He is talking about the attitude of violence. Here is the attitude of the servants – intensity, severity, and force, like the attitude of a tornado. The servant's focus and determination is to subdue and take dominion. This is serious even to the point of it equating with a miracle, unexplained at awe with your mouth wide open. To do things with our money like the servants that will put the world at awe with power and might is very significant, yet only according to our ability or dunamai and dunamis. Hence, some people are more powerful and mighty with their money than others. In other words, we ought to be doing mighty deeds with our money by force and with the attitude of a tornado! Here are some biblical examples of a dunamai and dunamis tornado attitude with money!

Pr. 31: 23-24

"Her husband is respected at the city gate, where he takes his seat among the elders of the land. She makes linen garments and sells them, and supplies the merchants with sashes." NIV

What is happening in this scene of the wife of noble character?

_____

_____

_____

Look at the position of the husband, venerated in the land because of what she is doing with her money and how she is using it. She is selling garments while supplying the merchants with sashes; it is as if she is performing miracles with communities in awe at her works. This household has dominion in this town or city because of her works. Why, her husband is highly venerated all over the neighborhoods, and she is adored.

Acts 10: 2

"A devout man, and one that feared God with all his house, which gave much alms to the people, and prayed to God always." KJV

What significant thing is this devout man doing with his money and why is he doing it?

_____

_____

_____

This devout man, named Cornelius, feared God with his entire house in prayer daily! He believed God had a purpose for him and his family's life. His worship to God involved his money. This devout man used his blessings to bless others, glorifying God, to meet the needs of people. He being a Roman army officer, he was in charge of a hundred soldiers. He must have been a very busy man, yet he took the time out to be venerated without his high authority. Why, he was a religious man and spent his money on people that were in need. No matter what your position is in life, true dominion only comes through our position in Christ Jesus. In addition, true dominion comes also from how we forcefully advance the Kingdom of God, with power and authority! Our authority is from Christ, and we reign in Him in our communities around us. Here are two ways to reign in Christ, through our giving and our living.

Write the initial C or V by the dunamis and dunamai characteristics of Cornelius and the virtuous woman.

Force (subdue)	_Might_
Miraculous power	_Mightily_
Ability	_Mighty deed_
Strength	_Mighty (worker or)_
Violence	_Mighty miracle_
Abundance	_Power_
	Mighty (wonderful) work

What are your views on money and are you dunamis and dunamai about your views?

_____

_____

_____

Are your views biblical? If so, how?

_____

_____

_____

Did your views on money change after doing this exercise? If so, how?

_____

_____

_____

In what ways did this exercise help enrich your marriage?

_____

_____

_____

Y

EXERCISE # 3

REVIEW QUESTION # 22 📖 DO YOU AGREE ON HOW TO BRING UP YOUR CHILDREN?

Our children are much a part of Kingdom building. In Gen. 1:28 to be fruitful and multiply is in the physical state. Yet in a two-fold commandment it is also a spiritual state. God commanded husbands and wives to be fruitful and multiply in the physical to have dominion in the physical and in the spiritual. Yet this dominion is designed with a holy stance, teaching our children they are spiritual beings, holy subduing physically and spiritually. Even today, our dominion is still physical and spiritual! First, our holy stance physically is our presence in the world under the power of our Lord and savior Jesus Christ, making Him known forcefully advancing, Matt. 11:12! Secondly, our holy stance spiritually is our presence in the world under the power of the Holy Spirit, defeating the principalities, powers, rulers of the darkness of this world and spiritual wickedness in high places, Eph. 6:

12! Therefore, we are to train up our children to take these stances in the Lord. Proverbs is a good book on training and bringing up children. Consequently, we will not spend a lot of time on this subject. However, at a subsequent time these matters will be discussing in more depth. Look at and read Pr. 3:11, 12, 12:1, 12:15, 13:24, 15:4 (teach your children respect and correct speech). Read Pr. 16:9 (teach your children how to be directed by the Lord), and 18:13 (teach your children to listen). Look at Pr. 18:21 (teach your children it is death and life in the power of the tongue. When you speak lies, hatred, and disobedience, you will eat it). Read Pr. 22:6 (this is an old time favorite of many churchgoing folks. Still, you can count on and rely on these promises from the Lord! Therefore, if you train them up right starting at an early age, no matter how far they stray, they will not depart and they will be back). Pr. 22:15, 23:13,14 is saying a beating will not kill the child; it will save his or her soul. In addition, the rod gives wisdom, however, the rod spared is the reason for so much crime among our children and young adults. Without God, there is no hope for them. The child has not received enough wisdom and not enough rod to give wisdom, Pr. 29:15. Finally, teach your children to put their trust in the Lord, it is for their safety, Pr. 29:25!

In what ways do these passages of Scripture help you with agreeing on bringing up your children?

EXERCISE # 4

REVIEW QUESTION # 23 📄 DO YOUR CHILDREN KNOW THAT IT IS FOOLISH TO TRY TO PLAY ONE OF YOU AGAINST THE OTHER?

Children are a very important part of enriching our marriages. Why, when they are unruly it disturbs and disrupts our home life and our marriage relationships. Teach your children, Eph. 6:1-3 and Ex. 20:12. The child needs to know what is honor and how it reflects; taking heed to what either parent may say or instruct. In addition, this includes the importance of listening to that parent and obeying them. Here is how the child can take dominion in the land and how they respect what their parents say. **Read Deut. 6: 4-8**

Put these steps in order according to the passage of Scripture.

THE CORRECT ORDER ⇨

Teach God's commandments to your children when they get up in the morning.

Know God's greatest commandment in your hearts.

Teach God's commandments to your children when sitting around the house.

Teach God's commandments to your children when they go to bed.

Teach God's commandments diligently to your children.

Teach God's commandments to your children when you are mobile.

Hear our one and only true God.

The second greatest commandment is like the first, to love your neighbor as yourself. We cannot forget this part of God's

122

commandment. In addition, for your children I would make sure they understand that everyone is their neighbor, including their parents. Tell them that loving their parents is as important as how they love themselves. Explain how we love ourselves. On that account, this is a way to honor their parents by obeying God's commandments. Obeying God's commandments loves God and loving your parents is honoring God.
[Answers 7, 2, 5,3,6,4,1]

How serious is the consistent teaching of Deut. 6:4-8 in your home?

_____

_____

_____

Are you going to renew in the pnĕuma of your mind these biblical methods of training up your children in the way they should go?

_____

_____

_____

How would this exercise enrich your marriage?

_____

_____

_____

Ŷ

EXERCISE # 5

REVIEW QUESTION # 25 ▤ DO YOU HAVE A GOOD RELATIONSHIP WITH YOUR IN-LAWS?

We need to leave our fathers and mothers, cleave to our spouse and become one flesh, Gen. 2:24. Our parents should not run our households under no circumstances. However, when it comes to building God's Kingdom our parents are a part of that. If our parents are not believers, we should be praying for their salvation. In addition, we need to love them, as we love ourselves, Matt. 22:39. If for any reason we have a problem loving our in-laws, I have a simple fact for you. God said you could love your in-laws as you love yourself. They are your neighbors. To love your in-laws as you love yourself is having respect for them. God commanded us to love our in-laws. Respect will go a long way, and this will help break down any uneasy feeling towards one another. Let us look at our duty we need to take with our in-laws. God's Word tells us to provide for our own relatives, I Tim. 5:8. Additionally, having this type of provision is not monetary only but also in word, in love and in good deeds. As husbands and wives, we have the responsibility to honor our parents. Our in-laws deserve our honor and respect as parents. Consider Jacob's relationship with his **father in-law Laban, Gen. 30:27-36.**

Laban and Jacob had a working relationship in verse 27. Laban was thankful and excited about their relationship. After all, Jacob did increase his earnings. How are we helping our in-laws financially? Moreover, as Jacob gave of himself Laban wanted to give back in verse 28. The point is in the relationship and their respect for one another. God will honor your respect for your in-laws. What does this have to do with subduing and having dominion?

Is it not how God blesses you, rather if it is monetary, like Jacob, or in respect, honor, and in duty, it is our God-given duty to respect, honor and love our in-laws. Here Christ is reigning through us in the lives of our in-laws. He is making himself present in their lives. *Furthermore, it is exhibiting God's love when we give ourselves to service, God is glorified, and His Kingdom is advancing!* Always keep this in mind that Christ Jesus reigns! Not only does He reign through life situations, events, and transcending into this world and in our lives, *He is reigning in us and through us.* **Review your memory verse on this subject in the NIV.** This is how His Kingdom is forcefully advancing, by reigning through his saints to take the gospel to a lost and dieing world. Mat. 11:12, Lk 16:16, 28: 18-20!

By allowing Christ to reign through us in the lives of our in-laws, what does this mean to you?

In your own words, how is this advancing the Kingdom by allowing Christ to reign through us in the lives of our in-laws.

_____

_____

What does this have to do with enriching your marriage by having a good relationship with your in-laws?

_____

_____

One way to look at this is that you will have peace in your surroundings and marriage when your in-laws are present in your lives and are led by God. See how a disruptive in-law can be stressful in a marriage, Gen. 31. Yet, if you have a disruptive in-law, God can make it right. Why, we see the power of God in this story in favor of his son Jacob. We are His children and He will make it right if we are obedient to Him. Let Christ reign through you, stay in prayer and watch God work in your situation. We can see how a little stress came upon the marriage in verses 14, 15, yet God prevailed in verses 16 and following. See how God came to Laban on behalf of Jacob to protect him from harm and danger in verse 24.

If you are having any problems with your in-laws, talk it over with your spouse and start to pray. Allow God to show you what you need to do as He did Jacob. Moreover, let God intervene and make it right.

REVIEW QUESTION # 27 📄 ARE YOU GLAD TO INTRODUCE YOUR SPOUSE TO FRIENDS AND ASSOCIATES?

We have discussed extensively about subduing and having dominion over the earth, and how building God's Kingdom has a lot to do with money, how we use it to the glory of God. Moreover, along with building God's Kingdom from the money aspect, there is a multiplication process. Under the multiplication and duplication process the great commission plays a huge part in building God's Kingdom, Mat. 28:18-20. Therefore, as believers we need to keep this in mind as we continue. **First, are we ashamed of each other? ☐ Yes or ☐ No. Please check the box ☑ that applies.** I hope the answer is no, especially after knowing our spiritual state of being is purity. We should not be ashamed of each other under any circumstances. The way our spouse looks, talks, or carries themselves should be dealt with if it is unspiritual. However, we need to be seeing each other as God sees us. (We covered this in chapter three). **Secondly, are we ashamed of something in our life? ☐ Yes or ☐ No.** Let me say this in plain English, are we hiding any past lifestyles and are ashamed to bring them out into the open? Just maybe your friends, peers, and associates know some things your spouse does not! I hope your answer is no because of whom we are in Christ Jesus we should not be ashamed of anything in the past or in the *present*; we are new creatures in Christ Jesus. I hope you are not involved in any unspiritual activities that keep you from introducing your spouse to any friends, peers, or associates. These things must be resolved immediately if this is the case. Why, sin must be dealt with; moreover, we are building God's Kingdom and we should be Kingdom-minded. When we are introducing our mates to friends, peers and associates, we are practicing the duplication and multiplication process under building God's Kingdom, subduing and having dominion over the earth. Our friends and associates need to see God's Kingdom in our relationships. In addition, if they are married, duplicate and multiply ourselves into our friends and associates lives under the great commission, teaching them the truths of God's Word and what a God-fearing relationship is as husband and wife. Additionally, if they are lost, focus on saving their souls. Read the great commission, Mat. 28:18-20. Are we excited enough about what God is doing in our marriage to go out and show the lost, especially our friends, peers and associates, what it is to be married and saved by the blood of Christ? Everything we have discussed and practiced up until this point in Truth About Marriage we really need to shine with radiance in our marriages. Christ Jesus has to be the radiance that people see in us. Your friends, peers, and associates should see something in you that they may need in their life and marriage. If there is something that you are ashamed of, you need to repent of it and put on the new you in Christ Jesus, Eph. 4:22-24. If you are ashamed of anything in your spouse's life, please express it now so your marriage can receive a renewal of the mind. Let us free our minds from anything that is holding us back from showing the world what God is doing and what His Kingdom looks like in our marriage. **If you have any, write down your shameful behaviors below, whatever you think about your spouse or of yourself.**

_____

_____

_____

Here are some Scriptures to combat your wrong thinking about yourself or your spouse. Here, you can be the examples you need to be among your peers, associates, church members, friends, and family. *(If you are in sin, go to the dynamic habitual change exercise in unit four.)* **Read Ph. 4:8, Ro. 8:9 and Ph. 3:13.**

Think of things about your spouse that are pure, praiseworthy, just, lovely, honest or honorable, and of good report. These things drove you to them when you first met. If you met under other circumstances, there are some things in Ph. 4:8 about your spouse that you can think of presently. **Write down what some of those things are below.**

_____

_____

_____

This will win people over to want what you have in Christ Jesus in dominion and power. **What is dominion and power in marriage?**

_____

_____

_____

It is a territory or sphere of influence and realm in your marriage. Dominion and power is Christ reigning in your marriage, and that gives you power and control to reign with Christ in confidence. Your marriage will show subduing power that will attract people's attention to wonder what is it that you have that they do not have. Christ Jesus' radiance attracts! It is the Christ that reigns through us, that is where we reign, subduing and having dominion over the earth and forcefully advancing the Kingdom, Mat. 11:12, Eph. 2:6, Gen. 1: 28.

Now we are at the point of duplication or multiplication. Here we want to give people what we have. People are going to want it for their marriage as well. Your marriage represents the Christ-Church and the Church-Christ relationship. We can teach others these principles to apply them in their marriage as well. Duplicate ourselves into the lives of others. This is a big part of marriage enrichment. By sharing our enriched lives in Christ Jesus our Lord and Savior, we bless others to enrichment in Christ Jesus!

UNIT VI

ONENESS BETWEEN ONE MAN AND ONE WOMAN

QUESTION EVALUATION REVIEW

QUESTION EVALUATION REVIEW ONE
BETWEEN ONE MAN AND ONE WOMAN

MEMORY

I Corinthians 7: 3-4

"Let the husband render unto the wife due benevolence [due her]: and likewise also the wife unto the husband. The wife hath not power of [over] her own body, but the husband: and likewise also the husband hath not power of his own body, but the wife." KJV

ONENESS BETWEEN ONE MAN AND ONE WOMAN

God intended for man and woman to be inseparable. He created one man for one woman, period! It is not two men or two women, as it was said earlier in chapter three. That is why God, knowing it was not good for man to be alone, Gen. 2:18, created a helpmeet whom might I say was a woman, not a man. Why, this was the only part of God's creation that was not good enough for Him. Therefore, God created woman, whom was named by man, Gen. 2: 23. In the same passage, it is apparent that the man and woman were inseparable!

Gen. 2: 23

"And Adam Said, This is now bone of my bones, and flesh of my flesh: she shall be called Woman, because she was taken out of Man. Therefore shall a man leave his father and his mother, and shall cleave unto his wife: and they shall be one flesh." KJV

One flesh! What does this mean to be one flesh? It means united as one. The man and the woman have now become one flesh or one body! Here, God's Word is precisely and unequivocally referring to sex. **(Review your memory verse for reference.)** Similarly, here is a Scripture reference of God's imperative and momentous instructions on inappropriate use of sex.

I Cor. 6: 15-16

"Know ye not that your bodies are the members of Christ? Shall I then take the members of Christ, and make them the members of a harlot? God forbid. What? Know ye not that he which is joined to an harlot is one body? For two, saith he, shall be one flesh." KJV

Inappropriate use of sex is obviously fornication or adultery. However, oneness between one man and one woman is quite naturally appropriate after leaving their father and mother in holy matrimony. In this chapter, we will explore the fun things about sex and foreplay. Sex in itself is putting all your problems, misunderstandings, pressures in life, bad feelings, likes, and dislikes behind you. Sex had none of these burdens in the beginning. If you want to have *heavenly* sex, what is heavenly sex? It is under total serenity of Christ. Where your mind is cloudless, clear, bright, untroubled, tranquil, calm, and peaceful by the power of the Holy Spirit! Here you are setting your affections (the affections of the mind) on things above not on the earth! From Col. 3: 2, KJV. Having sex as part of being free from the world and all its problems is who we need to be. Here is where you become totally under the control of the Holy Spirit and totally into your mate all at the same time. This is a powerful state of being. Why, being not ashamed in the Hebrew is in a pure and holy state of being. Yet in the flesh! You observe the beauty of the naked body in its full measure. Husbands and wives, you will have the most exciting, bountiful, sensational and memorable times sexually with your mate *guaranteed* only by the power of the Holy Spirit. God intended for sex to be enjoyable, not worn-out and undesirable. **Here is an example of enjoyment, exciting, bountiful, sensational sex and memorable times *guaranteed* in light of the truth**. It is very simple, Gen. 2: 25: *"And they were both naked, the man and his wife, and were not ashamed." KJV*. What is the biblical meaning of the word 'ashamed'? Here, it is from the Hebrew word **bûwsh** – *to be disappointed or delayed (be, make, bring to, cause, put to, with, a-) shame. Be (put to) confounded [related word – disconcerted] (-fusion), become dry, delay, be long.* This word 'ashamed' in the context of Scripture in meaning has a lot to do with the flesh and its oneness. Flesh, in its meaning they did not see each other in the flesh. Why, they were holy and pure. Oneness in its meaning they did not disappoint or delay one another sexually – verse 24, one flesh. In addition, their sex was not dry or had a long wait for sensation! They were not disconcerted, meaning frustrated, upset or having lack of confidence in one another. How so? They were perfect beings! 'Ashamed' was not anywhere in their vocabulary, activity or behavior. How wonderful, awesome, and powerful that must have been to live that way in every aspect of life. Make no mistake about it! We can live like this as well. On whose account, we have the power in Christ Jesus our Lord and Savior. I challenge you, do not let Satan deceive you like Adam and Eve to think otherwise. Notice the power is in God, not of yourself. Here is where Adam and Eve made the mistake, thinking the power was in themselves and not God, Gen. 3: 5. This is where the power starts, a not an ashamed life in **Ro. 8: 9.**

"But ye are not in the flesh, but in the Spirit, if so be that the Spirit of God dwell in you. Now if any man have not the Spirit of Christ, he is none of his." KJV

> DO YOU WANT TO HAVE JOYFUL, EXCITING, BOUNTIFUL, SENSATIONAL SEX AND MEMORABLE TIMES GUARANTEED IN THE LIGHT OF THE TRUTH? THEN SIT BACK, ENJOY AND GET INVOLVED IN ALL THE DISCUSSIONS IN THIS CHAPTER!

Before discussing these topics, go before the thrown room of God, asking Him to purify your heart and mind, surrendering yourself to Him to give Him the glory for your mate. Pray your mind will be free from sin, doubt, and any problems in life. Remember you are surrendering to Him totally. If you are in sin by any cause, you need to seek forgiveness from God. If you sinned against someone, go make it right and be reconciled to them and to God. You will not fully experience your sexual breakthrough! (We have previously covered and discussed this issue of forgiveness and sin; see Ask for Forgiveness when you do something wrong in chapter 2). *In addition, the passages used in this chapter are metaphoric and similes. Therefore, it is up to each believer's conviction based on the truth in Jesus Christ and how the spirit works in your heart and mind. Prayer in the spirit will lead you to believe truth based on His reproving and His interpretation, Jo. 16: 8, II Pe. 1:20.*

Ⴤ

EXERCISE # 1

REVIEW QUESTION # 7 🗐 DO YOU FOCUS ON THE THINGS YOU APPRECIATE ABOUT YOUR MATE AND EXPRESS APPRECIATION IN TANGIBLE WAYS?

Let us indulge in foreplay. Remember this is not a self-gratification test, but to gratify each other or to indulge each other. These acts are the start of foreplay, before the affectionate touching begins. The focus is not on the self but the other person, your spouse, and your love, your mate. They are the only person in your world right now. When you are together with your mate, they will have all of you and your agape, romantic and affectionate love! You are together all alone in an empty room that has become full to every extent of space with sweet, passionate love and **no one else in the world matters right now but**

you and your mate. 👤 🛏 👤

Circle the symbol or symbols that represent your sex life. Circle what you think goes after the equal sign. Then explain your answers or symbols below. You must be truthful and do not cover up your problems. Remember to have fun with these exercises. Yet, if it is too serious to handle right now, to adjust, put off your differences and be reconciled. Seek help from your brothers and sisters in Christ.

♥ + 👤 🛏 👤 =

🌪 ⚡ 🌧 🌨 🌦 🌥 ☼ ○ ☼ ☾ 🕊 🌎 ♿

🌬 👨‍👩‍👧 🏆 🏠 🏜 🏝 🏞 🎁 🚑 🕸 🔒 🍽

⚡ ☠ 💣 ☹ 😐 ☺ 👍 👎 👆 ✌ 👇

_____

_____

_____

_____

_____

_____

❒ Let us use God's Word to enhance our sex lives with our mates. The first passages of Scriptures are for the wives. This is the first day of appreciation, affectionately and sexually. Husbands, this is your day catered to the wives. Then, wives, on the next day practice your Scripture catering to your husband. Keep in mind this is the whole idea to put into practice what the Scripture has already laid out for us. Hence, this is a two-day exercise of fun and excitement. Husbands, your focus is going to be on what you appreciate about your wife affectionately. Wives and husbands, you need to be prepared because

134

these exercises can lead to sexual relations if you are serious about foreplay at this time. However, in your own way, take the time to practice what the Scripture has laid out for you. Read Solomon's song 7: 1-9. Let us pick out some verses to start with and focus on the things appreciated. I suggest going over these exercises first and then commencing to practice them precisely if you will. With respect to the exercise, you can also use your own style of foreplay while using God's Word as a guide. (If you understand the principles in these exercises, check the box ☑and continue.)

Day One

Husbands, you can appreciate your wife in Solomon's Song 7: 4-9. In addition, compliment your wife and express your appreciation tangibly. Here is my way of practicing God's Word affectionately and sexually. Learn how to appreciate your mate's body regardless of its flaws. Remember, you are a wonderful, precious, and beautiful spiritual being as a regard for yourself and your mate. In Christ Jesus, this is how He sees you in His Spirit! Therefore, see each other in the same light.

Sol. 7: 4b

"Your eyes are the pools of Heshbon by the gate of bath Rabbim." NIV.

Evidently, this must have been a beautiful place and a sight to see these pools of water. On that account, I can imagine seeing my wife's eyes as beautiful as the blue crystal clear waters of the Caribbean Seas. At this point, I will gaze into my wife's eyes and tell her how beautiful they are while my hand gently touches her face.

Sol. 7: 6-8

"How beautiful you are and how pleasing, O love, with your delights! Your stature is like that of the palm, and your breasts like clusters of fruit. I said, "I will climb the palm tree; I will take hold of its fruit. May your breasts be like the clusters of the vine, the fragrance of your breath like apples." NIV?

I will have to tell my wife how beautiful she is. I am well pleased with her appealing to me sexually. Husbands, describe your wife's breasts, how you enjoy them. In addition, how you would like to hold them in your hands and stroke and kiss them. Then gently put your face close to hers, as the fragrance of her breath is pleasant to your scent.

Sol. 7:9

"And your mouth like the best wine." NIV

After gently putting your face close to hers, kiss her passionately. Climb the palm tree and take hold of its fruits. At this point, husbands, you are now gently on top of your wife as you touch and feel her delights! The Scripture tells us how they are pleasing to you!

Husbands, if you do not like my approach, describe in your own words how you would put into practice these passages of Scriptures affectionately and sexually.

_____

_____

_____

_____

_____

_____

Husbands, select a time for you and your wife to come to an agreement, then practice the exercise. Remember what we talked about in the opening of this unit. Review first before you continue.

Wives, you can appreciate your husband in Solomon's Song 5: 11-16.
In addition, compliment your husband and express your appreciation
tangibly. Here is my way of practicing God's Word affectionately and
sexually. Learn how to appreciate your mate's body regardless of its
flaws. Remember you are a wonderful, precious, and beautiful spiritual
being as a regard for yourself and your mate. In Christ Jesus, this is
how He sees you in His Spirit! Therefore, see each other in the same
light.

Sol. 5: 12

**"His eyes are like doves by the water streams, washed in milk, mounted
like jewels." NIV**

Wives, look into your husband's eyes and tell him how gorgeous they are. Here,
you have a picture of pure white doves standing by fresh, lovely
waters. Milk is also pure white and jewels are perfect. His eyes are
pure white, not red or yellow, they are clear and beautiful to you.
Solomon appears to be a healthy man. Good health can give you
beautiful pure white eyes. This is a beautiful sight to gaze into your
mate's eyes and notice their perfection and beauty. Therefore,
wives, gaze into your husband's eyes passionately. If his eyes are
not as white as pearls, tell him you love them anyway. Remember
to learn to appreciate your mate's body regardless of its flaws. In
addition, husbands should not feel intimidated by Solomon's
stature and perfection.

Sol. 5: 13a

**"His cheeks are like beds of spice yielding perfume, NIV, as a bed of
spices, as sweet flowers." KJV**

Touch your husband's cheeks and tell him how handsome he is, as fresh as a
bed of spices, and as sweet as flowers yielding perfume.

Sol. 13b

"His lips are like lily's dripping with myrrh."

> Then tell him your lips are like lilies, dripping sweet-smelling myrrh and say, "I want to taste them."

Sol. 13:14b

"His body is like polished ivory decorated with sapphires."

> Tell your husband, "I want to rub you down with oil to see your body as polished ivory decorated in sapphires. With your muscles strong and masculine and your love sapphire, I want to satisfy you."

Sol. 13: 16a

"His mouth is sweetness itself; he is altogether lovely."

> Wives, now taste his lips like lilies dripping with myrrh and kiss his mouth of sweetness passionately while touching him down his body covered in oil.

Wives, if you do not like my approach, describe in your own words how you would put into practice these passages of Scriptures affectionately and sexually.

_____

_____

_____

_____

_____

Wives, select a time for you and your husband to come to an agreement, then practice the exercise. Remember what we talked about in the opening of this chapter. Review first before you continue.

How did you enjoy these exercises and how do you think your mate enjoyed them?

_____

_____

_____

In what ways does this exercise help enhance your relationship with your mate?

_____

_____

_____

EXERCISE # 2

REVIEW QUESTION # 11 DO YOU DO MANY DIFFERENT THINGS TOGETHER AND ENJOY BEING WITH EACH OTHER?

What are some things that you can think of to do together that will make a romantic evening? I can think of some things that will lead to the big prize!

The Big Prize

In exercise #1, did you pick the present for one of your symbols that represents your sex life? Sex can be a gift or a prize! A gift is something that you give and receive with excitement! Hence, the focus is not on you that is giving the gift but the person receiving the gift and the gift itself. The prize is to please the other person and to satisfy them. We should allow our sex life to be similar – the big prize. We give our mate our body to please them and to satisfy them, I Cor. 7: 3-4. It is more blessed to give than to receive, Acts 20: 35b. It should never be to gratify the person, giving primary

focus. On that account, a gift is to gratify the other person while in the process you feel good about giving. Therefore, you enjoy giving the big prize that makes you satisfied also. "Honey, you worked hard all week or all day so I have a gift for you – the big prize." Make no mistake about it; this is only another way to look at sex, it is not a rule. At times, you may feel like you have my spouse's body anyway, and it is not exciting to you anymore. Therefore, be creative with your sex life to spice it up.

With respect to the "Big Prize", going out on a romantic date or just to hang out together can impart some spice into the marriage. Going out on dates can lead to a mood of affection and anticipation to have sexual relations with your mate – the "Big Prize". Here is my idea of a date from Scripture. **Read Deut. 24: 5, Pr. 5:18**

Deut. 24: 5

"When a man hath taken a new wife, he shall not go out to war, neither shall he be charged with any business: but he shall be free at home one year, and shall cheer up his wife which he hath taken." KJV

Pr. 5: 18

"May your fountain be blessed, and may you rejoice in the wife of your youth." NIV

Husbands, we have a lot of work to do here. I suppose you could not take off work for a whole year to honeymoon your wife. I could not either. With that said, how can we practice God's Word with this particular passage of Scripture? I suggest, husbands, that we have a lot of dating to do. Dating is when we come together to enjoy each other. Dating also leads to wooing one another. The passages above are very clear on the importance of being and spending quality time together along with a wooing relationship. Husbands are to cheer up their wives, have fun and to rejoice in their wives of their youth (young and active). Husbands, your fountain has reference to from the word **mâqôr** – *source of water, even when naturally flowing; also of tears, blood (by euphemism of the female pudenda).* Therefore, husbands, in the context of Scripture *your fountain is your wife's genitalia as a mild or agreeable expression substituting the realistic expression a source* *of water that is flowing.* May your fountain be blessed, or may you enjoy to the fullness extent your wife's pudenda. Additionally, in order to keep our relationships with our mates young and active, we need to take time off from everything else in the world and spend time with our mates. Wives, you can also have a fountain from a female perspective in the Scripture. Your husband is to satisfy you with his fountain and to keep it young (your sex life). In turn, wives, keep your husband satisfied because his genitalia also belongs to you – your fountain. What does this have to do with dating? Remember the whole year you are supposed to have taken off from work to enjoy and to cheer up your spouse, let dating be part of your honeymoon that leads to sex. As the Scripture said, enjoy and cheer up one another. You can do things together that are fun and exciting then end your evening with

the "Big Prize! 🛏️ " ♥

What would you call a date with your mate? Here are some suggestions. Check the boxes ☑that you would like to do at least once a week. Then fill in the blanks with some suggestions of places to go.

☐I would like to go to the movies

_____

_____

_____

☐I would like to go out to dinner. _____

_____

_____

☐We can go out to play some games. _____

_____

_____

☐I would like to double date at times. (With who?) ___

_____

_____

☐We can go and have a picnic in the park. _____

_____

_____

❐ We can go and listen to some Jazz.

❐ We can go dancing.

❐What can you come up with as a day or evening out?

(Remember to keep it exciting. Chose places that you both can enjoy.)

In what ways does this exercise help your relationship with your spouse, including your sex life?

Ϋ

EXERCISE # 3

REVIEW QUESTION # 17 ▤ DO YOU ANTICIPATE SEXUAL RELATIONS WITH YOUR PARTNER?

What makes you anticipate sexual relations with your partner? Is it the fact that it is a gift from God? God created sex, husbands and wives should anticipate their sexual union with their mate. Sex is an innate drive created by God that needs to be controlled by the spirit. There are three states of beings combined with sex. There is a spiritual state of being, a mental state of being, and a physical state of being. In fact, we already covered all three states in the beginning of this chapter (see the beginning of this chapter as reference). We covered the spiritual state as not being ashamed. We covered the mental state as being free from the problems of the world and sin. Furthermore, we covered the physical state, appreciating your mate's body and expressing it in tangible ways. Remember, prayer is highly important to have heavenly sex (review the opening of this chapter). In addition, the man and the woman have sex to glorify God, not to seek self-gratification but intimacy and pure love between each other. The man and the woman aim to glorify God and to please one another. *"Whether therefore ye eat, or drink, or whatsoever ye do, do all to the glory of God." I Cor. 10: 31, KJV. (Having sex is to the glory of God!)*

I Cor. 7:3-5
"Let the husband render unto the wife due benevolence [her due]: and likewise also the wife unto the husband. The wife hath not power of [over] her own body, but the husband: and likewise also the husband hath not power of his own body, but the wife." KJV

Due benevolence in the Greek, benevolence is to reconcile, to be will minded and agree. Benevolence is duty, goodwill, to be charitable, meaning out of the kindness of your heart, without looking for anything in return. Not that you do not want to enjoy sex or expect to enjoy it. Sex is something that you do want and you do expect to happen. Why, it is innate! In plain English, you desire sex, but as a Christian not for self-gratification. You only want to please your mate. With this in mind, the relationship is an equal partnership in immeasurable excitement. The husband and the wife are excited in this union between one man and one woman. Moreover, in verse 4 it is clearly saying that neither man nor woman has power over their own body, but each has power over the other's body. The word 'power' in the KJV from the Greek means we do not have the freedom to exercise authority over our own bodies. In other words, we cannot keep ourselves from one another. If we do keep ourselves from one another, it has to be only for a time period that is consenting under prayer, I Cor. 7:5.

So there we have it, God's commandment to anticipate sexual relations with each other. Now let us look at some practical scenes of anticipation, transitioning from God's commandment to God's practical love scenes.

Let us take a look at God's Word, which is full of anticipating sexual relations that express love between one ⅋ husband and one wife ⅋ .

Sol. 5: 8

"I charge you, O daughters of Jerusalem, if ye find my beloved, that ye tell him, that I am sick of [from] love." KJV (The wife's anticipation)

⅋ What strikes you the most about this passage in light of anticipating sex, (this is the wife's anticipation)?

_____

_____

_____

Sol. 5: 1

"I am come into my garden, my sister, my spouse [bride]: I have gathered my myrrh with my spice; I have eaten my honeycomb with my honey; I have drunk my wine with my milk: eat, O friends; drink, yea, drink abundantly, O beloved." KJV (The husband's anticipation)

⅋ What strikes you the most about this passage in light of anticipating sex, (this is the husband's anticipation)?

_____

_____

_____

Sol. 2: 17

"Until the daybreak and the shadows flee away, turn, my beloved, and be thou like a roe or a young hart upon the mountains of Bether." KJV (The wife's anticipation)

⅋ Prepare for this, wives – your anticipation. First of all what does 'Roe' mean from many words in the Hebrew, two in particular are:

tsebîy – of prominence, splendor (as conspicuous), roe (-buck). In addition, roe also means from the Hebrew word **tsâbâh** – to amass, that is growing turgid. What is **turgid** – unnaturally distended, swollen. A roe is a young hart, a ram a stag or deer. This is incredible; she wants her husband to satisfy her beyond the natural. She anticipates an intensely sexual encounter with her husband! Come on now, a **roe** in the Hebrew, conspicuous, to amass. That is growing turgid! She wants him to be a **stag** (the adult male for various deer) in modern-day terms, a stud. A **stud** is a collection of horses and mares for breeding. A **stallion at stud** Available for breeding purposes – said of male animals. 'Stud' has many similarities to a 'roe'. Husbands, how are we going to keep up with this metaphoric love story? The metaphors here within these passages are stud and roe bound! On that account, the wives are looking for the husbands to have a mighty erection or an extended erection to satisfy them. A young hart is full of energy, a strong tower of lasting stimulation (until daybreak). Wives, this is your anticipation! Husbands, I suggest being in prayer! Be filled with the Holy Spirit and led by the spirit, (review the beginning of this chapter). Husbands, you can satisfy your wife, believe God and his word in prayer.

Wives, were you shocked to know this kind of language was in Scripture to enhance your sex life with your mate? What is your natural God-given innate feeling on this type of anticipation?

_____

_____

_____

_____

_____

Prov.5: 18

"May your fountain be blessed and may you rejoice in the wife of your youth." NIV

♀ Husbands, your fountain has reference too from the word **mâqôr** – source of water, even when naturally flowing; also of tears, blood **(by euphemism of the female pudenda)**. Therefore, husbands, in the context of Scripture your fountain is your wife genitalia as a mild or agreeable expression substituting the realistic expression of a source of water that is flowing. May your fountain be blessed, or may you enjoy to the fullness extent your wife's pudenda. What does blessed **(bârak)** mean in the context of Scripture? God is blessing man as a benefit, to profit the godly man as gaining an advantage with his wife's pudenda. In plain English, the godly man's wife's pudendum or vagina is valuable and paramount to him in sensation and sexual satisfaction. Husbands, you do not need masturbation, pornography, adultery, fornication, or any other sexual satisfaction other than your wife! Her pudendum or vagina takes supremacy over any other sexual stimulation.

♀ **Husbands, what comes to mind when you think about your wife's pudendum and how it is paramount in your life? What is your natural God-given innate feeling on this type of anticipation?**

_____

_____

_____

_____

♀ *Husbands and Wives* ♀

In what ways does this exercise enhance your marriage and how often do you want to have sex per week or month?

_____

_____

Y

EXERCISE # 4

REVIEW QUESTION # 18 ▤ ARE YOUR SEXUAL DESIRES COMPATIBLE?

Our sexual desires are innate created by God. Everyone's sex drive will not be the same. Hence, our eating habits and work habits are not all the same. Only the innate drives that are under the control of the Holy Spirit are right! Make no mistake about it; innate drives that are under the control of the Holy Spirit are healthy drives. While focusing on God, he can create a desire of greater anticipation and compatibility. God will not command something as we put forth the effort to complete it and not put in us the desire to carry it out.

Phi. 1:6.

[Being confident of this, that he who began a good work in you will carry it on to completion until the day of Christ Jesus, NIV.]

God's commandment in I Cor. 7: 3-5 is a work and our obligation. It takes a lot of work in our lives not to be selfish. Moreover, as any other commandment of God takes habitual practice, and God will carry it on to completion. This is a promise from God. Let us not be ashamed of what God created for us to enjoy. Consent to sex controlled by the Holy Spirit! We can count on God to bring us to a compatible sexual appetite and relationship as it was in the beginning, Gen. 2: 24-25. Man and woman's sexual compatibility as obviously seen in the lives of Adam and Eve, Gen. 2: 24-25, is inescapable. They were naked and not ashamed as one body! They were pure and holy! We must see each other this way in our spiritual state of being to look deeper into our compatibility... (Review Ro. 8:9). Let us look at our mates as wonderful, precious, spiritual beings. Additionally, We must believe God will carry us through to completion in sexual intercourse with our mate (especially men). Wives are harder to please so men we must work extra hard with habitual practice. One practice is for men to pray before sex with this in mind; God enhances your erection through the Holy Spirit. Your erection will stay hard and swollen *(roe)* long enough to please and satisfy your wife and glorify God in everything! In addition, men, if for any reason you climax first, do not stop or lose intenseness. Continue to be a roe as hard and strong as before. *Do not stop to enjoy it, please your wife first, allow her to climax and God will bring it to completion.* Your wife will be satisfied and you will too! Why, you have decided in your mind to be a stud under the power of the Holy Spirit! These are the desires of the husband and the wife who are sexual compatibility.

The Husband and the Wife

Let us look at some compatible examples, love scenes from the Word of God. The wife is the conductor in many passages in Solomon Songs. For example, the wife tells the husband to blow upon her garden that is south. She specifies the husband as the north wind blowing on her garden so her spices can flow out. Husbands and wives read Sol. 4: 16 and write down the metaphoric, simile language. After writing it down, the language tells you what it means to you.

Sol. 4:16

"Awake, O north wind; and come, thou south; blow upon my garden that the spices thereof may flow out. Let my beloved come into his garden, and eat his pleasant (precious) fruits." KJV

_____

_____

_____

_____

_____

I believe this has a strong intimate, passionate, and sexual indulgence. *The act of gratifying your mate non-selfishly, foreplay in preparation of intercourse. This passage of Scripture has a strong indication of oral sex. Yet I am not interjecting my thought into Scripture. Remember these passages are metaphoric and similes. Therefore, it is up to each believer's conviction based on the truth in Jesus Christ and how the spirit works in your heart and mind. Prayer in the spirit will lead you to believe truth based on His reproving and*

His interpretation, (Jo. 16: 8, II Pe. 1:20). After reading the above passage, let us now look at the next passage of Scripture, Sol. 5:1. This passage is after he has fulfilled his wife's request in 4:16. Complete this passage as the former.

Sol. 5:1

"I have come into my garden, my sister, my bride; I have gathered my myrrh with my spice. I have eaten my honeycomb and my honey; I have drunk my wine and my milk. Eat, O friends, and drink; drink your fill, O lovers."

_____

_____

_____

_____

_____

Read Sol. 7: 8, 10-13, 8:1-3. After husbands and wives have read these passages, explain in your own words the metaphor and simile and what they mean to you. Then describe how you can put these Scriptures into practice, the former and the latter, while planning your next evening together.

_____

_____

_____

_____

_____

In what ways does these exercises enhance your sexual relationship?

_____

_____

_____

EXERCISE # 5

REVIEW QUESTION # 19 📄 DO YOU FEEL FREE TO DISCUSS YOUR SEXUAL DESIRES WITH YOUR MATE?

What are sexual desires? Are they sexual whims, lust for sex or a hunger, longing and an appetite to please your mate? What is a **desire** in the Webster dictionary? *It is to wish or long for, to crave. To ask for; request, a sexual appetite; passion.* What is **lust**? *A very strong craving or desire. It is an intense sexual appetite. In addition, lust is to have an intense desire, or intense sexual desire.* **What kind of desires should you have for your mate?** *A sexually, longing for, a request for and a passionate appetite desire.* On the other hand, *lustful strong cravings, with an intense sexual appetite.* (Chose your answer and write it below.)

_____

_____

_____

Let us look at the difference more in depth. One is healthy and the other is not. A brother in Christ told me that it is OK to lust after your wife. I had to correct him on this matter. If for any reason you think it is OK to lust after your mate, there is a big difference between *lust* and *desire* after. **Lust** has an *intense* desire and can be a dangerous drive. Innate drives need a balance. The word **intense** means – *strained or exerted to a high degree. It is extreme in degree, concentration, or measure. You will put forth strenuous effort.* Whatever means possible is the conformed attitude with **lust**! Why, it comes from the root meaning of the word 'intense'. **Desire,** however, is just the opposite. *Desire just wishes for, request for, ask for, and longs for sex. It has an appetite for sex, a passion for sex.* What is having a **passion** for sex? This is the essential element to **desire**. *It is a fervent devotion or ardent sexual feelings and desire – love.* To have a **passion** for sex coupled with love that has restraints or control. Lust does not have control but extreme measures or strenuous efforts that can become out of proportion or wild in nature. This type of behavior is open for evil sexual desires that have no restraints. Therefore, be careful in exercising lust for your mate.

Let us look at God's Word for the true meaning to discuss sexual desires without them being lustful. Webster has a good spin on the word. However, in Deut. 21:11, in the Hebrew, the man's desire for his wife is **châshaq**. This Hebrew word means *to cling, join, to love, delight in or long. This is the desire we should have sexually for or mates.*

Why should we discuss our sexual desires? They build confidence with expectations to have sexual relations with our mates! Let us read the confidence and expectation the wife had for her husband in Solomon Songs. She knew what she had in a mate and was free to talk about her sexual desires and expectations.

Sol. 2: 17

"Until the daybreak and the shadows flee away, turn, my beloved, and be thou like a roe or a young hart upon the mountains of Bether." KJV

(Review exercise # three Sol. 2:17 section.)

We can read how confident the wife was about her expectations of her husband. She is asking him to be like a roe, a young stag. Here is the NIV translation.

Sol. 2:17

"Until the day breaks and the shadows flee, turn, my lover, and be like a gazelle or like a young stag on the rugged hills."

She asks her husband to be a roe until daybreak. Picture or envision your sexual relations as strong as a gazelle, roe, stag, or a stud (the modern-day usage of being like a roe). Why should we be afraid of using such language of metaphors and simile to describe our sexual desires? Are we afraid? We should not be afraid to explore the great things about sex and all its healthy pleasures. When we converse, it is a great way to start or envision our sexual adventures. Make it adventurous because it is exciting and fun to create memorable moments for the rest of your life!

♟ **Wives, in your own words describe your way of envisioning your husband to be a roe, gazelle, a young stag, or a stud. It could be for how long you so desire!**

_____

_____

_____

_____

♟ **Husbands, in your own words describe your way of envisioning yourself to be a roe, a gazelle, a young stag or a stud to your wife for however long you so desire!**

_____

_____

_____

_____

♟

I will go to the husband conversing with his wife of what he sees and desires of her sexually.

Sol. 7:6-9

"How beautiful you are and how pleasing, O love, with your delights! Your stature is like that of the palm, and your breasts like clusters of fruit. I said," I will climb the palm tree; I will take hold of its fruit." May your breast be like the clusters of the vine, the fragrance of your breath like apples, and your mouth like the best wine." NIV

♟ The Husband's sexual desire here is to take hold of his wife's fruits on her body like palm tree because they are delights! What are her fruits, metaphorically speaking? I would envision her breast, her pudendum, and her total stature. Solomon was obviously a breast man! Turned on by the breast, as are most men. In many intimate moments, the breast is the first place he would touch and kiss. The pudendum is another place to touch to excite his mate. Solomon's exclamation is to climb the palm tree and take control of the intimate moment. He said, *"I will take hold of its fruit."* **She was all for it. Look at her response to her lover.**

Sol. 7:11-12

"Come, my lover, let us go to the countryside, lit us spend the night in the villages. Let us go early to the vineyards to see if the vines have budded, if their blossoms have opened, and if the pomegranates are in bloom there I will give you my love." NIV

This is true love and the flames are rising high by their conversation. The metaphors and similes are hot and on fire. Listen to these: vines budded, blossoms have opened, and pomegranates are in bloom – there I will give you my love. She is ready for love and her fire is in flaming for sex.

Husbands, in your own words, how can you hold a conversation with your wife to make her ready for sex, or in modern-day terms 'hot ✿ for sex'?

_____

_____

_____

_____

Wives, in your own words, what can your husband say to get you ready for sex or hot ✿ for sex? What would turn you on without your husband touching you?

_____

_____

_____

_____

👤 In what ways does this exercise enhance your sexual discussions? 👤

_____

_____

_____

👤 How would you teach other couples the advantage of enjoying sex by just conversing in preparation or sharing just your desires? 👤

_____

_____

_____

THE SEXUAL UNION

SCRIPTURE

SESSION

She invites him for a night of love and passion filled with sexual delicacies, including the pleasure of her breasts.

Sol. 7: 11-13

"Come, my lover, let us go to the countryside, let us spend the night in the villages. Let us go early to the vineyards to see if the vines have budded, if their blossoms have opened, and if the pomegranates are in bloom there I will give you my love. The mandrakes send out their fragrance, and at our door is every delicacy, both new and old, that I have stored up for you, my lover." NIV

"O That thou wert as my brother, that sucked the breasts of my mother! when I should find thee without, I would kiss thee; yea, I should not be despised." KJV

This section of the book is explosive. I believe there is no reason why two people that have been joined together by God should not live until death do you part. If you want to enjoy this sexual union to the fullest, the practice of the first five chapters is paramount in your marriage. However, this sexual union is what binds the husband and wife as one! Without this in your marriage, you really do not have a true marriage under God, with the exception of catastrophic events that warrants you not able to have sex. Taking this unit seriously is vital to your marriage and will give you a successful one.

Conclusion

TURNING RELATIONSHIPS INTO HOLINESS

When we turn relationships into holiness, it is to allow Jesus Christ to be at the center of our marriage. You will not have a successful marriage without Him. John 15:5: *"I am the vine and you are the branches, He who abides in Me and I in him, bears much fruit, for without Me you can do nothing."* **This is why the Truth is Jesus Christ in your marriage!**

Truth about Marriage will teach you How To
- Love your wife as Christ loves the Church.
- Be heads over your households.
- Submit to your own husbands.
- Use the bible to determine your convictions, decisions, and practices in life in general and marriage in particular.
- Study the bible, pray, worship God, and seek to serve God together.
- Seek to please one another.
- Ask for forgiveness when you have done something wrong (not just saying, "I am sorry").
- Focus on the things you appreciate about your mate and express appreciation in tangible ways.
- Have biblical communication and communicate on a daily basis.
- Be excited with each other.
- Show love in many different tangible and practical ways.
- Court one another by occasional gifts, unexpected attention etc.
- Have pleasant and friendly conversations.
- Pray for one another. Support and seek to encourage one another.
- Anticipate sexual relationships with your partner to have heavenly sex. (Set your affections on things above, not on things on the earth, Col. 3:2.)
- Be as one with finances
- Multiply, subdue and build God's Kingdom/having dominion over the earth.

"I hate divorce," says the Lord God of Israel, "and I hare a man's covering himself with violence as well as with his garment," says the Lord Almighty, NIV.

Be blessed and prosperous in everything you do, from J.J. Hairston.